WRITING SHORTER LEGAL DOCUMENTS

Strategies for Faster and Better Editing

SANDRA J. OSTER, PH.D., JD

Cover design by Elmarie Jara/ABA Publishing.

Printed in the United States of America.

15 14 13 12 11 5 4 3 2 1

Library of Congress Cataloging-in-Publication Data
Oster, Sandra Jean.
   Writing shorter legal documents : strategies for faster and better editing /
Sandra J. Oster.
      p. cm.
   Includes index.
   ISBN 978-1-61632-991-4
1. Legal composition. I. Title.
   KF250.O848 2011
   808'.06634—dc23

                                                            2011023174

Discounts are available for books ordered in bulk. Special consideration is given to state bars, CLE programs, and other bar-related organizations. Inquire at Book Publishing, ABA Publishing, American Bar Association, 321 North Clark Street, Chicago, Illinois 60654-7598.

www.ababooks.org

In memory of my sister Harriette Oster

Table of Contents

Acknowledgments

In appreciation to my sister Rose Bloom and her husband, my brother-in-law Arthur, for their unflinching support and encouragement and their comments on an earlier draft of this handbook. Attorney Clair Miller and my former legal assistant Anne Buck have also been steadfast and encouraging, and they provided excellent comments on an earlier draft.

I thank all of the attorneys and scientists for whom I have edited documents over the years, especially in the last decade—with a special thank you to Paul Cordo, Ph.D., neuroscientist and biomechanical engineer. I honed my editing skills at their expense. Their trust in my language, editing, and linguistic abilities and knowledge allowed me to experiment with writing and editing strategies.

A sincere thank you to Erin Nevius, Executive Editor at American Bar Association Book Publishing, who shares with the ABA and me a desire to help attorneys develop a style of writing that does not obscure their meaning and that helps them communicate as clearly as possible to the wide variety of audiences that they encounter every day in the practice of law.

Introduction—
A Section That You
Really Need to Read

At some time or another, as a lawyer, a legal assistant, or a law student, you may need to shorten a legal document in order to improve its readability and to clarify its text, to free up space for additional information, to make information easier for readers to access and retrieve, or to meet length requirements that may be specified by a court or another recipient. It is the rare legal document that does not need editing. The legal documents written by the author of this handbook are no exception.

Writing Shorter Legal Documents gives you editing strategies to help you shorten the text of legal documents and illustrates how to apply the strategies, with examples taken from actual legal documents. You can also use these strategies to help you develop a more concise and clearer style of writing.

In 1999, the American Bar Association passed a resolution urging agencies to use plain language in writing regulations. Plain language is also a virtue in most other legal documents besides regulations. Applying the editing strategies in this handbook will also help you develop a plain-English writing style that readers can readily understand.

Criteria for selecting text-shortening strategies. The text-shortening strategies in this handbook were selected, based on: (a) the capacity of the strategy to promote a clear, precise, and direct style of writing—that is, to promote plain English, (b) the impact that each strategy has on reducing the total number of lines, words, or characters in a paragraph, (c) the ease with which lawyers, paralegals, and law students will be able to implement the strategy, and (d) the capacity of the strategy not only to promote the readability of the legal document but also to enhance your credibility as a legal professional.

As used in this handbook, *readability* involves the amount of effort, time, and concentration that a reader needs to exert in order to understand the text. You need to aim for high readability. In other words, you need to aim for producing a text that meets length requirements and that does not require much reading effort for readers to readily understand the content and to quickly locate and retrieve information from the document.

Credibility relates to believability: Does the reader find the writer credible? You need to aim for high credibility. You need to come across as a legal professional who is honest and highly knowledgeable in law, who knows how to apply law (and which law) to the facts of the case, and who wants the readers to understand the legal document and its message without much effort. And all this needs to happen usually within a prescribed document length and by an inflexible deadline.

Overview of chapters. This handbook has five chapters. Two of the most frequently applied strategies are in Chapter 2 (Strategy 1) and Chapter 5 (Strategy 30). Strategy 1 covers the selection of terminology, and Strategy 30 addresses the elimination of redundant or unnecessary information. However, there are many other ways to shorten the text of legal documents, and Chapters 2–5 explain some of them.

Chapter 1 gives an approach for you to shorten the text of legal documents. Without giving approach much thought, most writers start at the beginning of sections and paragraphs and work down the page, looking for something to take out. Or they select individual sentences to shorten, without giving much thought to how the shortening of that one sentence will affect the total length of the paragraph. Revising sentences at the beginning of a paragraph or revising isolated sentences often does not affect length. Chapter 1 explains an approach that will help you to apply the text-shortening strategies in Chapters 2–5 efficiently and successfully.

Chapters 2 and 3 present some key text-shortening strategies that focus on revising features of language—vocabulary, phrases, and sentences—and on modifying lists within and across sentences. The more features of a clear legal style that you know and can recognize, the more you will able to revise your vocabulary, phrases, and sentences in order to meet length requirements of legal documents. The features of legal vocabulary, phrasing, and sentence structure that are discussed in Chapters 2 and 3 will help you recognize and revise features of language that affect document length.

Chapter 4 gives text-shortening strategies that change the layout of text on the page through the manipulation of white space that visually defines paragraphs, sections, and lists. In most cases, the strategies in Chapter 4 need to be applied consistently across paragraphs, to give the same look to each page of the document and to help make the organization of the document clear to the readers.

Chapter 5 offers ways to cut content. Writers will often cut content only as a last resort, after they have tried shortening sentences and still find the document too long or the total word count too high. However, at times cutting content is unavoidable and requires tough decisions. Chapter 5 gives strategies to help writers identify content that can be cut without substantially changing information in the document.

Relationship between the suggested strategies and submission requirements. Almost all of the text-shortening strategies in this handbook can be applied to most types of legal documents, regardless whether the recipient is the court, another attorney, an employee, a client, or the editor of a law journal. However, a few strategies might not be appropriate for all federal and state courts, or law journals, depending on their submission requirements for legal documents, and a few might not be appropriate for all lawyers, judges, and other audiences of legal documents due to their preconceptions about legal language. Therefore, the more you know about your readers and the submission requirements for your type of legal document, the more you can confidently select particular text-shortening strategies. Where particular text-shortening strategies in this handbook run counter to submission requirements from a federal or state court, or a law journal, you should not apply them.

> *You need to double-check that each text-shortening strategy from this handbook that you want to apply does not violate submission requirements.*

Examples in this handbook. *Writing Shorter Legal Documents* primarily uses examples from actual public legal documents to illustrate the application of its text-shortening strategies. Extended examples are presented in tables, which are numbered sequentially in the handbook, and shorter examples are included within the textual discussion of length-shortening strategies. The examples used in this handbook may have been modified in the following ways:

(1) **Single-spaced text.** Most examples are single-spaced for printing economy, but many were double-spaced in the original.

(2) **Justification.** All examples appear with ragged right-hand justification even though the originals may have been flush-right. This change, implemented to assist readability, did not change the length of the examples in terms of the total number of lines, words, or characters.

(3) **Line length.** The examples in tables bear the line lengths in the original documents, unless otherwise noted.

(4) **Font.** Examples in tables are mainly in Helvetica 7-point Regular font, except for passages in tables that are in **Helvetica 7-point Bold Oblique font** for emphasis. Examples integrated within the text of this handbook are in ***Times 10-point Bold Italic font***.

(5) **Corrected errors.** The editing term *[sic]* is not used in any of the examples. Typographical errors, misspellings, and gross grammatical errors in the original, if any, have been corrected.

(6) **Footnotes.** Footnotes, if any, have been omitted from the examples.

(7) **Superscripted numbers.** In examples longer than one sentence, each sentence begins with a superscripted number for reference.

(8) **Additional modification.** Sometimes examples have been otherwise modified to better illustrate a point about language and how to shorten a legal document.

Sources from which the examples were taken. The legal documents from which examples in this handbook were selected are listed below. They were chosen according to the following criteria: (a) except for Document 6, they are public documents accessed through periodic internet searches during 2010, with the last access on January 16, 2011; (b) their style reflects particular features of legal writing that the text-shortening strategies address; and (c) their subject matter may capture the readers' interest.

In the tables and examples, the source of each excerpt is identified by "Doc." and a number that corresponds to one of these numbered documents:

(1) *Berg v. Obama.* Complaint for Declaratory and Injunctive Relief, Preliminary Statement (8th District Pennsylvania n.d.). (http://www.scribd.com/doc/5021983/Berg-v-Obama; accessed January 16, 2011)

(2) *Bundy v. Florida*, 471 So. 2d 9 (Fla. 1985). Court denied appeal by appellant from conviction of first degree murder and from trial judge's imposition of death sentence after jury recommended death. (http://www.law.fsu.edu/library/flsupct/59128/op-59128.pdf; accessed January 16, 2011)

(3) *Demjanjuk v. Holder*, Submission in Response to Court's Stay of Removal, April 16, 2009 Order (6th Cir. April, 2009). (http://www2.nationalreview.com/dest/2009/05/06/7 1694f722e5a5d7c8e4aff8d948e40c4.pdf; accessed January 16, 2011)

(4) *Doe v. Doe.* Petition for Custody. Case No. Omitted. Accessed January 16, 2011 on the internet.

(5) *Exxon Shipping Co. v. Baker* (9th Cir. 2007). Brief for the Pacific Coast Federation of Fishermen's Associations and the Institute for Fisheries Resources, as Amici Curiae in

Support of Respondents. (http://www.abanet.org/publiced/ preview/briefs/pdfs/07-08/07-219_RespondentAmCu 2FishermansAssocs.pdf; accessed January 16, 2011)

(6) *The Oregon Clinic Employee Handbook*. Updated September 2010. Portland, Oregon.

(7) *Rodearmel v. Clinton* (D.C. Columbia). Opposition to Defendant's Motion to Dismiss and Plaintiff's Memorandum in Support of His Cross-motion for Summary Judgment. (http://www.judicialwatch.org/files/documents/2009/ Rodearmel-OppMotionSJ.pdf; accessed January 16, 2011)

(8) *Sec. and Exch. Comm'n v. Madoff*, Plaintiff's Memorandum of Law in Support of Its Application for Emergency Preliminary Relief Against Defendants. (http:// docs.justia.com/cases/federal/district_courts/new_york/ 1:2008cv10791/336993/15; accessed January 16, 2011)

(9) *Sec. and Exch. Comm'n v. Madoff* (2008). Local Rule 6.1 Declaration of Alexander M. Vasilescu in Support of Plaintiff's Emergency Application for Temporary Restraining Order, Preliminary Injunction, Asset Freeze and Other Relief. (http://docs.justia.com/cases/federal/district-courts/ new-york/nysdce/1:2008cv10791/336993/14/0.pdf; accessed January 16, 2011)

(10) *Texas Beef Group v. Winfrey*, 201 F.3d 680 (5th Cir. 2000). Court affirmed lower court's ruling "that no knowingly false statements were made by the appellees [Winfrey, Harpo Productions Inc., and others]." (http://www.studentweb.law .ttu.edu/cochran/Cases%20&%20Readings/Business%20 Torts/oprah.htm; accessed January 16, 2011)

(11) *United States v. Kaczynski* (D.C. Montana 1996). Arrest Warrant/Affidavit for 'Alleged' Unabomber Ted Kaczynski.

(www.lectlaw.com/files/case07.htm; accessed January 16, 2011)

(12) *United States v. Kaczynski* (9th Cir. California 2001). Court affirms lower court's denial of Kaczynski's motion to vacate his conviction. (http://ftp.resource.org/courts.gov/c/F3/239/239. F3d.1108.99-16531.html; accessed January 16, 2011)

(13) *United States v. McVeigh*, 153 F.3d 1166 (10th Cir. 1998). Court affirms McVeigh's conviction and sentence. (http:// law.uark.edu/documents/Bailey_BE_US_v_McVeigh.pdf; accessed January 16, 2011)

(14) *United States v. Powers,* (Middle District, Orlando Division, Florida, 2008), Case no. 6:07-cr-221-Orl-31KRS. (http://www .flmd.uscourts.gov/notableCases/Opinions/USA-v-Powers .pdf; accessed January 16, 2011)

(15) *United States v. Marcus Schrenker.* U.S. District Court. Northern District of Florida, Pensacola Division. 2009. Affidavit of John P. Allen, in support of criminal complaint. (http:// www.ticklethewire.com/wp-content/uploads/2009/01/fake -plane-crash-affidavit.pdf; accessed January 16, 2011)

(16) *United States v. Stewart and Bacanovic*, 03 Cr. 717 (S.D. N.Y. 2003). Memorandum opinion in which the court denies Government's application for two subpoenas duces tecum, except for the proposed subpoena to Martha Stewart's attorneys for certain billing records. (http://fl1.findlaw.com/ news.findlaw.com/hdocs/docs/mstewart/usmspb122903opn .pdf; accessed January 16, 2011)

(17) *White v. National Football League* (U.S. Court of Appeals 8th Cir. 2009). Appellants appeal a Michael Vick Order in which the district court ruled that bonus payments were already earned and thus not subject to forfeiture. (http://

caselaw.findlaw.com/us-8th-circuit/1496110.html; accessed January 16, 2011)

(18) *Craigslist, Inc., v eBay, Inc.* (Superior Court of the State of California, County of San Francisco, 2008). Complaint for unfair and unlawful competition, false advertising, California trademark infringement, breach of fiduciary duties, and other causes of action. (http://blog.craigslist.org/etc/craigslist.vs.eBay.pdf; accessed January 16, 2011)

Legal- and non-legal-writing authorities. The more features of good legal- and nonlegal-writing styles that you know and can recognize, the more you can shorten legal documents with the approach explained in Chapter 1. In addition to legal-writing authorities that your state bar or others may recommend, the following references provide information on legal and non-legal writing that can help you develop an acceptable, conservative writing style:

The Bluebook: A Uniform System of Citation (2005). 18th Ed. New York: Columbia Law Review Ass'n. (aka *The Bluebook*)
The Chicago Manual of Style, 15th Ed. The University of Chicago Press (2003). (aka *Chicago Style Manual*)
Garner, Bryan A. (2001). *Legal Writing in Plain English: A Text with Exercises*: University of Chicago Press.
Garner, Bryan A. (2009). *Modern American Usage.* New York: Oxford University Press.
Garner, Bryan A. (2006). *The Redbook: A Manual on Legal Style*, 2nd Ed. Thomson/West.
Publication Manual of the American Psychological Association (2009). 6th Ed. Washington, D.C.: American Psychological Ass'n. (aka *APA Style Manual*)

Sabin, William A. (2005). *The Gregg Reference Manual, A Manual of Style, Grammar, Usage, and Formatting*, 10th Ed. McGraw Hill.

Strunk, William, White, E.B., and Angell, Robert (1999). *Elements of Style*. 4th Ed. Longman.

http://www.plainlanguage.gov

Chapter 1

An Approach to Shorten Legal Documents

This handbook offers an approach and strategies for shortening legal documents and for developing a concise writing style. The approach is presented in this first chapter, and then the editing strategies in Chapters 2–5 will help you execute the approach by making you more aware of characteristics of words, phrases, and sentences that can affect the length of documents. As used in this handbook, the term *legal document* covers a wide range of documents, including pleadings, courts' written opinions, business documents, and correspondence to attorneys and clients.

Step 1. Determine whether your legal document is under any submission constraints.

Whether your personal writing style is concise or wordy, you need to know whether your legal document is under any submission constraints in terms of length. Some documents might be under length constraints in terms of: (a) the total page

1

length, (b) the total word count, (c) the total number of characters, or (d) any combination of (a) to (c).

For example, Rule 32 from the Federal Rules of Appellate Procedure specifies the maximum length of briefs, appendices, and other papers. Interestingly, it addresses length in terms of **both** the total maximum number of pages and the maximum number of words: "A principal brief may not exceed 30 pages, or a reply brief 15 pages, unless it complies with Rule 32(a)(7)(B) and (C) . . . " and "A principal brief is acceptable if: it contains no more than 14,000 words; or it uses a monospaced face and contains no more than 1,300 lines of text." This rule goes on to mention that: (1) "A reply brief is acceptable if it contains no more than half of the type volume specified in Rule 32(a)(7)(B)(i)"; (2) headings, footnotes, and quotations count toward the word and line limits; but (3) the table of contents, certificates of counsel, and other items do not count toward the limits. In addition, the certificate of compliance must state the number of words or the number of lines of single-spaced type in the brief.

A brief for an *Amicus Curiae* in Support of the Plaintiff, Petitioner, or Appellant submitted to the Supreme Court of the United States is limited to 9,000 words.[1]

The Illinois Appellate Court (First District) limits a supplemental brief to 20 pages.[2]

Rule 8.204 from the California Rules of Court specifies length limits of a brief:

---

1. Fed. R. App. P. 33, page 44; Brief for an Amicus Curiae in Support of the Plaintiff, Petitioner, or Appellant, or in Support of Neither Party, on the Merits or in an Original Action at the Exceptions Stage (see Rule 37.3).

2. It is limited to 20 pages unless the party files a motion seeking additional pages in advance of the filing of the supplemental brief (see Fed. R. App. P. 38B.)

(1) A brief produced on a computer must not exceed 14,000 words, including footnotes. Such a brief must include a certificate by appellate counsel or an unrepresented party stating the number of words in the brief. The person certifying may rely on the word count of the computer program used to prepare the brief.

(2) A brief produced on a typewriter must not exceed 50 pages.

(3) The tables, a certificate under (1), and any attachment under (d) are excluded from the limits stated in (1) or (2).

(4) A combined brief in an appeal governed by rule 8.216 must not exceed double the limits stated in (1) or (2).

(5) On application, the presiding justice may permit a longer brief for good cause.

Some documents are obviously under no constraints except for those that you or your employer imposes, such as letters to clients, employee handbooks, and settlement proposals. In such cases, you may want to use the text-shortening strategies in this handbook to develop a concise writing style, shorten the length of such documents, and make them more inviting to read. While you may not have specific restrictions on a document, developing a readable writing style can help you win cases and clients.

Step 2. Apply text-shortening strategies to a stable draft of a legal document.

For efficiency, you need to revise a ***stable draft*** of your legal document. A stable draft is one that does not need many changes to its content, organization, and layout, and the changes that it does need are not extensive.

Waiting to shorten a paragraph until after the draft becomes stable will save you time and energy. It is a waste of time, for example, to work on reducing a wordy sentence, only later to omit the entire paragraph in which the sentence occurs.

Step 3. Apply the *paragraph-backwards revision approach* to shorten documents under submission constraints that limit the total number of pages.

You may have noticed that when you edit only the first few lines of a paragraph, the total length of the paragraph does not often change. Likewise, the text-shortening strategies in this handbook, when first applied individually or in combination to the initial or middle lines of a paragraph, might not result in the elimination of an entire line.

In the *paragraph-backwards revision approach*, you can shorten the text by following at least the first 2 procedures here:

(1) Identifying paragraphs with *short last lines*. A short last line of a paragraph ends closer to the left-hand margin than to the right-hand margin.

(2) Applying one or some of the editing strategies in the chapters of this handbook to the last two to four lines of the paragraph. In most instances, by focusing revision efforts on the end of a paragraph with a short last line, you can eliminate the last line. By applying these two procedures to multiple paragraphs with short last lines, you can change the total page length, or at least you can shorten it by enough characters to apply the third procedure.

(3) If the short last line of the paragraph still remains after you have edited the last two to four lines of the paragraph, work further *backwards* in the paragraph and apply the editing strategies in this handbook to the middle lines of the paragraph, and then to the first lines of the paragraph. The last line of the paragraph usually disappears.

(4)   If you still need to reduce the length of the paragraph or document, apply the ***paragraph-backwards revision approach*** to paragraphs with long last lines (i.e., paragraph with a last line that ends closer to the right-hand than to the left-hand margin), or eliminate content (Chapter 5).

The effect of the ***paragraph-backwards revision approach*** on the length of a document can be seen in Table 1. Application of a text-shortening strategy (in this case, Strategy 1) to sentence 3 in Table 1A results in the phrase ***with respect to*** being changed to ***regarding***—a change that eliminates the short last line of the paragraph, as shown in Table 1B.[3] However, notice that application of this same text-shortening strategy to only line 1 does not affect paragraph length, as shown in Table 1C, although it does reduce the total word count by two words.

Keep in mind: strategies to reduce the total number of words or characters in a document can be applied at any point in a paragraph to help you develop a more concise writing style. However, to effect a change in the total number of pages, you need to revise many paragraphs by first targeting the last few lines of each paragraph and then working backwards, toward the beginning of the paragraph.

Clarity is paramount. If the application of a strategy in this handbook decreases the clarity of the text, you should not apply it. Also, emphasis of particular information may be important in your legal argument. If the application of a strategy changes the emphasis in a way that you do not want, you should not apply the strategy.

---

3. A case could be made that the repetition of ***With respect to*** in Table 1 is emphatic. However, ***With respect to*** is repeated 5 times in the 6-page memorandum opinion, which counters the selective use of the term for emphasis.

Table 1. Use of the Paragraph-Backwards Revision Approach to a Paragraph.

Examples **A–C** are discussed in Chapter 1. Example **D** is discussed in Chapter 3 (Strategy 24).

A. Original Text. From Doc. 16. Total line count: 11, Total word count: 89, Total character count: 606

[1]*With **respect to** attorneys' notes or materials prepared in connection with representing Martha Stewart during the Government's investigation preceding the indictment in this case, the Government has not made an adequate showing of the need for any of the documents requested. [2]For at least four of the categories of documents, Government lawyers were involved in the communications in question and have their own notes. [3]**With respect to** the fifth category—documents concerning communications with Peter Bacanovic—Wachtell, Lipton has submitted an affidavit stating **that** it possesses no such documents.

B. A Revision: Application of the Paragraph-Backwards Revision Approach. Total line count: 10, Total word count: 87, Total character count: 600

[1]***With respect to*** attorneys' notes or materials prepared in connection with representing Martha Stewart during the Government's investigation preceding the indictment in this case, the Government has not made an adequate showing of the need for any of the documents requested. [2]For at least four of the categories of documents, Government lawyers were involved in the communications in question and have their own notes. [3]***Regarding*** the fifth category—documents concerning communications with Peter Bacanovic—Wachtell, Lipton has submitted an affidavit stating **that** it possesses no such documents.

C. Another Revision That Does Not Affect Paragraph Length. Total line count: 10, Total word count: 87, Total character count: 600

[1]***Regarding*** attorneys' notes or materials prepared in connection with representing Martha Stewart during the Government's investigation preceding the indictment in this case, the Government has not made an adequate showing of the need for any of the documents requested. [2]For at least four of the categories of documents, Government lawyers were involved in the communications in question and have their own notes. [3]***With respect to*** the fifth category—documents concerning communications with Peter Bacanovic—Wachtell, Lipton has submitted an affidavit stating ***that*** it possesses no such documents.

D. Further Revision for Strategy 1 Discussion. Total line count: 10, Total word count: 86, Total character count: 595

[1]***Regarding*** attorneys' notes or materials prepared in connection with representing Martha Stewart during the Government's investigation preceding the indictment in this case, the Government has not made an adequate showing of the need for any of the documents requested. [2]For at least four of the categories of documents, Government lawyers were involved in the communications in question and have their own notes. [3]***With respect to*** the fifth category—documents concerning communications with Peter Bacanovic—Wachtell, Lipton has submitted an affidavit stating it possesses no such documents.

Chapter 2

Revising Terminology to Shorten Legal Documents

Strategy 1. Replace longer, non-key terms with shorter synonyms.

Strategy 2. Use clear pronouns and pro-verbs.

Strategy 3. Use abbreviations for selected terms.

Strategy 4. Change nominalizations into their derived verbs and adjectives.

Strategy 5. Use verbs instead of nouns.

Strategy 6. Reduce redundant pairs of legal terms.

Strategy 7. Use the space at ends of lines.

Strategy 8. Shorten expressions of purpose.

Strategy 9. Use numerals for cardinal numbers greater than one.

Strategy 10. Punctuate and hyphenate conservatively.

Strategy 1

Replace longer, non-key terms with shorter synonyms

Most key terms should not be replaced with synonyms. Key terms are the vocabulary items that indicate the main topics and themes under discussion. Most key terms should be repeated throughout the text since readers rely on them to follow the topics and themes across sentences, paragraphs, and sections. Particularly in contracts, key terms should also be used consistently so that the terms on which the parties agree are as clear as possible; for instance, describing a property in different instances as "the building," "737 North Ave.," and "the warehouse" leads to ambiguity.

In contrast, non-key terms can be replaced with synonyms. Non-key terms do not indicate the main topics and themes under discussion, but provide relational or background information not central to the discussion. Replacing non-key terms with shorter synonyms can reduce the total line, word, or character count.

Two types of longer, non-key terms can be safely replaced with shorter synonyms:

(1) **Relational non-key terms.** These terms, often prepositional phrases, show semantic relationships among nouns,
verbs, adjectives, and adverbs. Table 2A gives examples
of relational non-key terms and their shorter synonyms.

(2) **Non-key terms for background information.** The
second group of longer terms is comprised mainly of
nouns, verbs, adjectives, and adverbs that are *non-key*
terms. Examples of these terms are in Table 2B.

By replacing unnecessarily long, non-key terms with shorter
synonyms, you can improve two problems that plague legal writing: legalese and elegant variation. *Legalese* is a style of language characterized by multiple, unnecessarily technical legal
terms without definitions. Lay readers often do not understand
technical legal terms, so legalese becomes an impediment for
lay readers who find themselves in need of understanding legal
documents. Some of the terms in Table 2A are words that char-
acterize legalese, such as *aforementioned* and *heretofore*, and
in Table 2B, *facilitate* and *altercation*.

To achieve clarity and a text that engenders high readability,
you also need to avoid *elegant variation*. Elegant variation is
the use of different, long synonyms for the same term, especially
a key term. With different synonyms referring to the same key
concept in one document, readers can become misled into think-
ing there are different main topics or themes under discussion,
rather than just synonyms being used for the same concept.

Fiction writers, rightly so, use elegant variation to compose interesting prose; without elegant variation, writing can
be repetitive. However, variation has no place in legal documents. Lawyers sometimes use elegant variation to show that
their vocabulary is large, sometimes to avoid boring readers, and
sometimes to vary vocabulary for no reason except to vary it.

All of these reasons cannot justify the extra textual length—and sometimes the lack of clarity—that elegant variation creates. Instead of using elegant variation, in most cases you need to repeat the same key terms throughout the document.

Readers of legal documents are concerned with content. The size of your vocabulary is irrelevant. The issue of boredom is also irrelevant; readers are not reading legal documents for entertainment. They want information from legal documents, and they do not want to exert much time and energy figuring out your meaning; they do not want to wade through extra words.

In Chapter 1, the example in Table 1 illustrates the replacement of the non-key term ***with respect to*** with its shorter synonym ***regarding*** to shorten the text. The examples in Tables 3A and 4A also illustrate how replacing longer non-key terms with shorter synonyms can shorten the text. In Table 3A, the non-key term ***regarding*** in sentence 3 can also be replaced by the shorter synonym ***about***, resulting in a reduction of just four characters, which is sufficient to eliminate the short last line of the paragraph, as shown in Table 3B. In Table 4A, the longer key term ***children*** is used in sentence 3, but the shorter key term ***child*** is used later in the sentence and in the paragraph. All of these sentences discuss children generically, not any particular child. In Table 4B, ***children*** (sentence 3) is replaced by ***child*** since ***child*** is used in the rest of the paragraph. Also, the replacement of the longer, non-key term ***at the time of*** (sentence 2) with ***when*** (sentence 3), plus grammatical changes due to the use of ***when***, results in the elimination of the short last line of the paragraph. Notice in this example, the ***paragraph-backwards revision approach*** is applied to sentences earlier in the paragraph than the last two to four lines since revision to these last lines will not eliminate the last line of the paragraph.

Table 2. Examples of Longer, Non-key Terms and Their Shorter Synonyms.

A. Longer, non-key terms and their shorter synonyms, in terms of the number of words or characters. **B.** Longer, non-key terms for background information and their shorter synonyms.

A. Longer, Non-key Terms and Shorter Synonyms

accordingly	thus, given
additionally	also, further
aforementioned	previous
a large number of	many, quite a few
alternatively	or, instead, in contrast
any and all	all
approximately	about
at that point in time	when, then
at the time of, at the present time, at present	when, now, currently
because	due to
because of the fact that	because, because of, due to
by means of, through the instrumentality of	by, through
by reason of	because of, due to
by virtue of	by, due to, because of
concerning	about
despite the fact that	although, even though
due to the fact that	due to, because, because of
during the time that/of, in the meantime	during, while, when
either . . . or	. . . or
fewer in number, more in number	fewer, more
for the period of	for
for the purpose of	for (however, see Strategy 8)
forthwith	now
frequently	often
heretofore	before, since
in accordance with	according to

in addition to	besides (negative connotation), also
in connection with	related to
In light of the fact that	given, considering
in order for	for (however, see Strategy 8)
in order to	to (however, see Strategy 8)
in relation to	regarding, concerning
in the amount of	for
in the course of	during, while
in the estimated amount of	about
in the event that, if the situation should arise that	if
in the matter of	about, concerning
in the majority of cases	usually, mainly
in the midst of	during, while
in view of the fact that	because, since, given
inasmuch as	since
including but not limited to	including
is able to	can
it is often/frequently/seldom the case that	often, frequently, seldom
it is possible that, the possibility exists that	perhaps, might, may, likely
on account of	due to, because, since
on the grounds/basis that	because, due to
on the order of	about
on the other hand	in contrast
on the topic of	regarding, about
or in the alternative	or
over the course of	over
pertaining to	about, regarding, for
prior to, preceding	before
provided that	if
regarding	about
said (e.g., the **said** person)	omit (e.g., this person)

subsequent to, following	after
subsequently	after, next, then
the color purple	purple
the sum total	the total, the sum
until such time as	until, when
until the time when	until, when
up to this point in time	until, since
with reference to	about, concerning, regarding
with respect to	regarding, about

B. Longer, Non-key Terms for Background Information and Shorter Synonyms

altercation	fight
assist	help
cognizant of	know, is aware
employ	use
exhibit	show
facilitate	help, aid
learned counsel	attorney
utilize, utilization	use

Table 3. Shorter Synonyms for Longer, Non-key Terms to Eliminate the Last Short Line of a Paragraph.

A. Original Text. From Doc. 8. Total line count: 7, Total word count: 85, Total character count: 555

[1]Through the investment advisor services of BMIS, Madoff has conducted a Ponzi scheme, whereby he has falsely represented to investors that returns were being earned on their accounts at BMIS and that he was investing in securities for their accounts. [2]In fact, Madoff, as evidenced by his admissions on December 10, 2008 to his Senior Employees, paid earlier investors with funds raised from later investors. [3]By concealing this activity from investors, Madoff made materially false statements *regarding* the source of the returns on investors' accounts.

B. Revised Text. Total line count: 6, Total word count: 85, Total character count: 551

[1]Through the investment adviser services of BMIS, Madoff has conducted a Ponzi scheme, whereby he has falsely represented to investors that returns were being earned on their accounts at BMIS and that he was investing in securities for their accounts. [2]In fact, Madoff, as evidenced by his admissions on December 10, 2008 to his Senior Employees, paid earlier investors with funds raised from later investors. [3]By concealing this activity from investors, Madoff made materially false statements *about* the source of the returns on investors' accounts.

Table 4. Shorter Synonyms Substituting for Longer, Non-key Terms.

Examples **A** and **B** are discussed in Strategy 1; Example **C** is discussed in Strategy 9.

A. Original Text. From Doc. 1. Total line count: 15, Total word count: 229, Total character count: 1249

[1]If in fact **Obama** was born in Kenya, the laws on the books **at the time of his birth** stated if **a child** is born abroad and one parent was a U.S. Citizen, which would have been his mother, Stanley Ann Dunham, **Obama's mother** would have had to live **ten (10)** years in the U.S., **five (5)** of which were after the age of **fourteen (14)**. [2]**At the time of Obama's birth**, his mother was only **eighteen (18)** and therefore did not meet the residency requirements under the law to give her son (Obama) U.S. Citizenship. [3]The laws in effect **at the time of Obama's birth** prevented U.S. Citizenship at the birth of **children** born abroad to a U.S. Citizen parent and a non-citizen parent, if the citizen parent was under the age of **nineteen (19) at the time of the birth of the child**. [4]**Obama's** mother did not qualify under the law on the books to register **Obama** as a "natural born" citizen. Section 301(a)(7) of the Immigration and Nationality Act of June 27, 1952, 66 Stat. 163, 235, 8 U.S.C. §1401(b), Matter of S-F- and G-, 2 I & N Dec. 182 (B.I.A.) approved (Atty. Gen. 1944). [5]**Obama** would have only been naturalized, and a naturalized citizen is not qualified and/or eligible to run for Office of the President. U.S. Constitution, Article II, Section I, Clause 4.

B. Revised Text. Total line count: 14, Total word count: 219, Total character count: 1201

[1]If in fact *Obama* was born in Kenya, the laws on the books *when he was born* stated if *a child* is born abroad and one parent was a U.S. Citizen, which would have been his mother, Stanley Ann Dunham, *Obama's mother* would have had to live *ten (10)* years in the U.S., *five (5)* of which were after the age of **fourteen** (14). [2]*When Obama was born*, his mother was only *eighteen (18)* and therefore did not meet the residency requirements under the law to give her son (Obama) U.S. Citizenship. [3]The laws in effect *at that time* prevented U.S. Citizenship at the birth of a *child* born abroad to a U.S. Citizen parent and a non-citizen parent, if the citizen parent was under the age of *nineteen (19) when the child was born*. [4]*Obama's* mother did not qualify under the law on the books to register *Obama* as a "natural born" citizen. Section 301(a)(7) of the Immigration and Nationality Act of June 27, 1952, 66 Stat. 163, 235, 8 U.S.C. §1401(b), Matter of S-F- and G-, 2 I & N Dec. 182 (B.I.A.) approved (Atty. Gen. 1944). [5]*Obama* would have only been naturalized, and a naturalized citizen is not qualified and/or eligible to run for Office of the President. U.S. Constitution, Article II, Section I, Clause 4.

C. Another Revision, Focusing on Numbers. Total line count: 13, Total word count: 214, Total character count: 1156

[1]If in fact *Obama* was born in Kenya, the laws on the books *when he was born* stated if *a child* is born abroad and one parent was a U.S. Citizen, which would have been his mother, Stanley Ann Dunham, *Obama's mother* would have had to live *10* years in the U.S., *5* of which were after the age of *14*. [2]*When Obama was born*, his mother was only *18* and therefore did not meet the residency requirements under the law to give her son (Obama) U.S. Citizenship. [3]The laws in effect *at that time* prevented U.S. Citizenship at the birth of a *child* born abroad to a U.S. Citizen parent and a non-citizen parent, if the citizen parent was under the age of *19 when the child was born*. [4]*Obama's* mother did not qualify under the law on the books to register *Obama* as a "natural born" citizen. Section 301(a)(7) of the Immigration and Nationality Act of June 27, 1952, 66 Stat. 163, 235, 8 U.S.C. §1401(b), Matter of S-F- and G-, 2 I & N Dec. 182 (B.I.A.) approved (Atty. Gen. 1944). [5]*Obama* would have only been naturalized, and a naturalized citizen is not qualified and/or eligible to run for Office of the President. U.S. Constitution, Article II, Section I, Clause 4.

Strategy 2

Use clear pronouns and pro-verbs.

Personal pronouns, demonstrative pronouns, and pro-verbs are shorter substitutes for longer terms that precede them. Their use can help you avoid repeating terms and can also help you shorten the text, since pronouns and pro-verbs use fewer characters and sometimes fewer words than do their antecedents. An *antecedent* is the term that precedes the pronoun or pro-verb, and to which the pronoun or pro-verb refers. These lists present personal and demonstrative pronouns and pro-verbs.

Personal Pronouns	**Demonstrative Pronouns**	**Pro-Verbs**
he, him, his, she, her, hers, it, its, they, them, theirs, you, your, I, me, mine, we, us, ours	*this, these, that, those*	*do so, does so, did so, will do so*

Pronouns and pro-verbs should be used *only if* the resulting text is clear; every pronoun and pro-verb needs an unambiguous antecedent. In Table 5A, no pronoun is used in the paragraph.

However, the personal pronoun *his* can be used in sentence 3 instead of repeating *Mauro M. Wolfe* since *his* is clear; there is no other singular, masculine noun to which *his* can refer in the preceding text. Replacing *Mauro M. Wolfe's* with *his* results in the elimination of the short last line of the paragraph and a reduction of three words.

A demonstrative pronoun points to a word or concept in the immediately preceding text. If the antecedent to a demonstrative pronoun is clear, you can use a demonstrative pronoun to shorten the text. In Example 1, *this* in the second sentence unambiguously refers to the hypnosis subject's response of pleasing the hypnotist; there is no other logical antecedent in the first sentence.

Example 1
These authorities reveal that hypnosis subjects are often so susceptible to suggestion and receptive to the hypnotist's verbal and nonverbal communications that *they may respond in accordance with what they perceive the desired response to be in order to please the hypnotist. This* may even occur in response to implicit stimuli unintentionally emanated from the hypnotist.

From Doc. 2.

A demonstrative pronoun that can logically refer to more than one concept in the preceding text needs to be revised for clarity. Clarity can be rescued by repeating the antecedent, which technically changes the demonstrative pronoun into a demonstrative adjective. In the second sentence of Example 2A, the antecedent to *this* is not readily apparent; it can refer to the *inference*, *divided loyalties*, or the restriction *could not have*, so *this* needs to be revised. In Example 2B, *prohibition* is added to *this*, clarifying the term *this prohibition*.

Text-shortening strategies cannot compromise clarity, and in this instance, the text in Example 2 was not shortened.

Example 2

A. [1]From the beginning of our Constitution, our forefathers inferred a person running for Office of the President could not have divided loyalties. [2]***This*** was a result of people coming from England to the United States who owed loyalties to both England and the United States.

From Doc. 1. Total word count: 45, Total character count: 273

B. [1]From the beginning of our Constitution, our forefathers inferred a person running for Office of the President could not have divided loyalties. [2]***This prohibition*** was a result of people coming from England to the United States who owed loyalties to both England and the United States.

Total word count: 46, Total character count: 285

Text can also be shortened through the use of a pro-verb if the antecedent to the pro-verb is clear. In Example 3A, the second sentence uses the pro-verb ***do so***, which ambiguously refers to ***avoid*** or ***find***. Due to this ambiguity, the appropriate verb should be repeated, as shown in Example 3B.

Example 3

A. [1]Thus, in order ***to avoid*** this plain language interpretation, Defendants ask the Court ***to find*** an ambiguity in an otherwise unambiguous clause of the Constitution. [2]The Court need not ***do so***.

From Doc. 7. Total word count: 31, Total character count: 189

B. [1]Thus, in order *to avoid* this plain language interpretation, Defendants ask the Court *to find* an ambiguity in an otherwise unambiguous clause of the Constitution. [2]The Court need not *avoid a plain language interpretation*.

Total word count: 34, Total character count: 221

Once again, text-shortening strategies cannot compromise clarity.

Table 5. Use of Clear Pronouns to Shorten the Text.

The phone number is changed from the original.

A. Original Text. From Doc. 9. Total line count: 5, Total word count: 56, Total character count: 341

8. [1]At approximately 3:45 p.m., I spoke with Madoff's attorney, Mauro M. Wolfe, Esq., and told him the Commission would seek this emergency application this afternoon in this Court. [2]I also told the attorney that I would contact him and requested that he be available in person or telephone. [3]***Mauro M. Wolfe's*** telephone number is (212) 777-7777.

B. Revised Text. Total line count: 4, Total word count: 53, Total character count: 328

8. [1]At approximately 3:45 p.m., I spoke with Madoff's attorney, Mauro M. Wolfe, Esq., and told him the Commission would seek this emergency application this afternoon in this Court. [2]I also told the attorney that I would contact him and requested that he be available in person or telephone. [3]***His*** telephone number is (212) 777-7777.

Strategy 3

Use abbreviations for selected terms.

As you know, an abbreviation is a shortened form of a term. There are different types of abbreviations; one type is comprised of the first and last letters of a word, such as *Ass'n* for *Association*.[1] An acronym, a type of abbreviation that is treated and pronounced like a word, is comprised of the first letters of the main words in a phrase, such as *PETA*, an acronym for the organization *People for the Ethical Treatment of Animals*. Another type of abbreviation is an initialism, comprised of the initials of a phrase and pronounced according to the initials. The initialism *U.S.A.* stands for the *United States of America*. Abbreviations can reduce the total number of lines in a paragraph and the total word count in a document.

---

1. *The Bluebook: A Uniform System of Citation* T.6 at page 335 (Columbia Law Review Ass'n et al. eds., 18th ed. 2005).

(a) When to use abbreviations. If "substantial space will be saved and the resulting abbreviation is unambiguous,"[2] an abbreviation for a key term can be consistently used throughout a legal document. However, clarity is not the only writing issue you need to consider before using an abbreviation.

Most abbreviations are more abstract than the longer terms they represent. As abstractions, abbreviations might negatively affect the readability of the text, especially when multiple, different abbreviations are used in a paragraph. Therefore, the use of abbreviations needs to be orchestrated.

You should abbreviate only those key terms that (a) are *frequently* used in the text, such as four or more times, or (b) are not frequently used in the text but their abbreviations are so common that they take on a concrete association with a physical entity, such as *U.S.A.* for *United States of America* and *C.E.O.* for the person in the role of *chief executive officer*.

(b) How to form abbreviations. If a standard abbreviation exists (standard as recognized by a legal-writing authority, such as *The Blue Book*), it should be used instead of a nonstandard abbreviation. For example, in text (not in a citation), the standard abbreviation *U.S.* (not *US*[3]) can be used as an adjective, such as in *The U.S. position remains unchanged*, but it needs to be written out when used as a noun,[4] such as in *Their entry into the United States was video-taped*.

If a term does not have a standard abbreviation, you can create an abbreviation to save space. Or if you are writing a legal document that does not need to conform to a legal standard, you can create an abbreviation.

---

2. *Id.*, at page 72.

3. *Id.*, at page 73.

4. *Id.*

An abbreviation is typically formed from: (a) the beginning letters of the term if the term consists of just one word, such as ***condo*** for ***condominium***; (b) an initialism (that is, the first letter of each main word comprising the term, such as ***GV*** or ***GPV*** for ***grandparent visitation***); or (c) the beginning and ending letters of a term, with the omitted letters replaced by an apostrophe, such as ***s'holder*** for ***shareholder***.

Periods and apostrophes are usually needed for abbreviations in legal documents submitted to a court or another entity that has explicit requirements for punctuation in abbreviations[5] (except for those abbreviations that are acronyms or common initialisms). For legal documents submitted to audiences without such requirements, periods are not usually used unless for clarity, since even periods add characters and may increase the length of a line and, thus, the length of a paragraph.

(c) When and how to introduce abbreviations. An abbreviation, whether standard or non-standard, is usually first introduced in parentheses and sometimes also in quotations immediately after the first mention of the targeted term, such as ***("ICE")*** for ***U.S. Immigration and Customs Enforcement*** (Table 28A) and ***("Wachtell, Lipton")*** for ***Wachtell, Lipton, Rosen & Katz*** (Table 22A). However, the quotation marks are not needed. Their omission can reduce the number of characters in a line of text and, thus, the length of the line of text, which might ultimately affect the length of the paragraph.

Once introduced, the abbreviation is used consistently throughout the remainder of the document. You do not reintroduce the abbreviation in later sections of the document, unless needed later for clarity or readability. For instance, if you

---

5. *Id.*, which can, by extension, be applied to apostrophes.

have not used an abbreviation in several pages and it is highly esoteric, you could introduce the entire phrase again.

Different abbreviations should not be used for the same term. Also, for readability, abbreviations are not often used in headings to sections and in titles to visuals. If an abbreviation is a common term, such as *FBI* for *Federal Bureau of Investigation*, or a common measurement unit, such as *min* for minute or *cm* for *centimeter*, the abbreviation, on its first mention, can be used without your first introducing it in parentheses after the term. The abbreviation can save characters and may ultimately affect the length of the line of text, the length of the paragraph, and the length of the document.

Strategy 4

Change nominalizations into their derived verbs and adjectives.

A nominalization is a noun that is the idea of a verb or an adjective. As such, a nominalization is more abstract than its derived verb or adjective. A nominalization has a distinctive ending, such as:

+tion	+ence	+icity	+ment	+ness
+sis	+ency	+ity	+ent	+hood

For example, the noun ***amendment*** is the nominalization for the verb ***amend***; ***correspondence*** is the nominalization for the verb ***correspond***; ***authenticity*** is the nominalization for the adjective ***authentic***; ***spoliation*** is the nominalization for ***spoil***; and ***crudeness*** is the nominalization for the adjective ***crude***. By rephrasing nominalizations into their derived verb and adjective forms, especially the first time the concept is used in the text, you can reduce the length of the text, and the text can become less abstract.

A nominalization, due to its grammatical ending, uses more characters than the verb or adjective from which it is derived. In addition, a nominalization is often preceded by *the* and followed by *of*, which also makes a sentence with a nominalization wordier than a sentence phrased with the derived verb or adjective. Table 6A gives a few nominalizations with their usual prepositions, and Table 6B gives their derived verbs and adjectives.

Examples 4A, 5A, and 6A use the nominalized phrases *the abduction of*, *the approval of*, and *the voluntariness*. Examples 4B, 5B, and 6B give their shorter, verb- and adjective-related revisions.

Example 4
A. During that time, Pete has not had any time alone with the baby, and the total number of hours Pete has had the baby with *the assistance of his family* comes to about 152 hours.

From Doc. 4. Total word count: 35, Total character count: 177

B. During that time, Pete has not had any time alone with the baby, and the approximate total number of hours Pete has had the baby comes to approximately 152 hours when *his family assisted*.

Total word count: 34, Total character count: 188

Example 5
A. The FDA imposed such a ban, with *the approval of* the cattle industry, only months after the Oprah Winfrey Show.

From Doc. 10. Total word count: 20, Total character count: 111

B. The FDA imposed such a ban, *which the cattle industry approved*, only months after the Oprah Winfrey Show.

Total word count: 18, Total character count: 105

Example 6

A. This court issued a *certificate of appealability*. The government submits that Kaczynski is foreclosed from *raising the voluntariness of his plea* on collateral review because he did not do so on direct appeal, but we conclude on the merits that the district court did not err.

From Doc. 12. Total word count: 46, Total character count: 276

B. This court issued a *certificate of appealability*. The government submits that Kaczynski is foreclosed from *using his voluntary plea* on collateral review because he did not do so on direct appeal, but we conclude on the merits that the district court did not err.

Total word count: 44, Total character count: 263

A nominalization is not typically revised into its derived verb or adjective form in two situations:

(1)   **The nominalization is a standard term.** If a nominalization is a standard legal term, it is not revised. For example, in Table 7A, the nominalizations *discretion* and *consideration* in the context of sentence 3 would not be revised since they are standard legal terms. Likewise, *certificate of appealability* in Example 3A is the name of a legal document, so *appealability* would not be revised. However, in Table 7A, *execution* in sentence 3 and *obligation* in sentence 4 are not

necessarily standard legal terms. Table 7B shows the nominalizations in sentences 3 and 4 rephrased into their derived verb forms. These changes reduce the text by two words.

(2) **The nominalization closely follows its derived verb or adjective form.** In a paragraph, when a nominalization closely follows its derived verb or adjective, the nominalization does not need to be revised. Example 7 illustrates this use of the nominalization *inference* in sentence 4, which closely follows its derived verb *inferred* in sentence 1.

Example 7

[1]From the beginning of our Constitution, our forefathers *inferred* a person running for Office of the President could not have divided loyalties. [2]This prohibition was a result of people coming from England to the United States who owed loyalties to both England and the United States. [3]Our forefathers did not want a person with dual loyalties to be able to secure the position as President of the United States. [4]*This inference* is taken from Article II, Section I, which plainly states qualifications for Office of the President must be a "natural born" citizen.

From Doc. 1.

Table 6. Examples of Nominalizations and Concise Counterparts.

Many phrases with nominalizations can be replaced with shorter phrases. **A.** Phrases with nominalizations (in bold italics). **B.** Verb or adjective from which the nominalization is derived.

A. Wordy Phrases with Nominalizations	B. Derived Verbs and Adjectives
coldness	cold
conclusion	conclude
conduct an *investigation* of, the *investigation* of	investigate, study
have the *capability* to	can, is able to
our *discussion* concerned	discuss
do/make/perform/give an *analysis* of	analyze
have an *expectation* of, the *expectation* of, there is the *expectation* of	expect, anticipate
in *combination* of, combine together	combine
In *consideration* of	consider
leads to the *speculation* that	speculate
make a *decision* about	decide
make a *reference* to	refer to
the *maintenance* of	maintain
offer a *suggestion* about/concerning, is *suggestive* of	suggest
results in an **increase/decrease** in	increase, decrease
the *speculation* that	speculate
take into *consideration*, the *consideration* of	consider
voluntariness	voluntary

Table 7. Allowing Some Nominalizations, Revising Others.

A. Original Text. From Doc. 17. Total line count: 11, Total word count: 152, Total character count: 925

[1]In 2004, Vick negotiated a contract with the Atlanta Falcons to play football for the team through 2014. [2]In addition to a yearly salary, the contract included two roster bonuses—one for 2005 ($22.5 million) and one for 2006 ($7 million). [3]The contract stated that the bonus amounts would be additional *consideration* for the *execution* of the long-term player contract, provided that (1) Vick adhered to all contract provisions and (2) Vick was on the Falcons' eighty-man roster on the fifth day of the 2005 and 2006 league years. [4]The contract also gave the Falcons the *discretion* to guarantee the bonuses for skill and stated that, if so guaranteed, Vick had an *obligation* to execute a new contract setting forth the terms of the skill guarantee. [5]The Falcons subsequently exercised their right to guarantee the bonuses for skill. [6]Vick met the roster provisions in the contract and was accordingly paid $29.5 million.

B. Revised Text. Total line count: 11, Total word count: 150, Total character count: 921

[1]In 2004, Vick negotiated a contract with the Atlanta Falcons to play football for the team through 2014. [2]In addition to a yearly salary, the contract included two roster bonuses—one for 2005 ($22.5 million) and one for 2006 ($7 million). [3]The contract stated that the bonus amounts would be additional *consideration* for *Vick's executing* the long-term player contract, provided that (1) Vick adhered to all contract provisions and (2) Vick was on the Falcons' eighty-man roster on the fifth day of the 2005 and 2006 league years. [4]The contract also gave the Falcons the *discretion* to guarantee the bonuses for skill and stated that, if so guaranteed, Vick *was obligated* to execute a new contract setting forth the terms of the skill guarantee. [5]The Falcons subsequently exercised their right to guarantee the bonuses for skill. [6]Vick met the roster provisions in the contract and was accordingly paid $29.5 million.

Strategy 5

Use verbs instead of nouns.

In Strategy 4, the verb form of a nominalization was shown to shorten the text. In general, using a verb instead of its noun will often shorten a sentence. This feature is especially evident in terms of homographs.

A homograph is a word that is spelled identically to another word but is different in grammar and sometimes in meaning. In the following word pairs, one homograph is a verb and the other, a noun.

to charge—the charge	*to insert—the insert*
to contract—the contract	*to plan—the plan*
to dye—the dye	*to play—the play*
to envelope—the envelope	*to schedule—the schedule*
to experiment—the experiment	*to total—the total*
to interview—the interview	*to transport—the transport*
to stop—the stop	*to purchase—the purchase*

In most instances, you should use the verb form of a homograph since the noun form results in a wordier sentence. For example, sentence 4 in Table 8A uses the homograph *interview* as a noun. The sentence is revised in Table 8B with *interview* used as a verb, which reduces the total word count and also eliminates the short last line of the paragraph.

Table 8. Use of the Verb Form of a Homographic Pair to Shorten the Text.

A. Original Text. From Doc. 11. Total line count: 10, Total word count: 111, Total character count: 654

[1]On April 3, 1996, your affiant and other agents of the FBI, ATF and United States Postal Service began the execution of a search warrant on the residence of Theodore John Kaczynski, located in Lewis and Clark County. [2]The premises is a one-room cabin, approximately 10 feet by 12 feet with a loft and without electricity or running water. [3]I am informed by other agents that records of Lewis and Clark County indicate that this property was purchased by Theodore John Kaczynski and another person in 1971. [4]*I am also informed by other agents that interview of neighbors revealed* that Kaczynski has lived at this residence by himself since that date.

B. Revised Text. Total line count: 9, Total word count: 106, Total character count: 633

[1]On April 3, 1996, your affiant and other agents of the FBI, ATF and United States Postal Service began the execution of a search warrant on the residence of Theodore John Kaczynski, located in Lewis and Clark County. [2]The premises is a one-room cabin, approximately 10 feet by 12 feet with a loft and without electricity or running water. [3]I am informed by other agents that records of Lewis and Clark County indicate that this property was purchased by Theodore John Kaczynski and another person in 1971. [4]*Other agents who interviewed neighbors informed me* that Kaczynski has lived at this residence by himself since that date.

Strategy 6

Reduce redundant pairs of legal terms.

Many pairs of legal terms, such as ***last will and testament***, ***null and void***, and ***cease and desist,*** developed in legal English after 1066 when the Normans invaded England. These pairs consist of an English term (e.g., ***will***) and the same term in French (e.g., ***testament***). Through the pairing of an English term with a French term, the British masses, most of whom spoke only English and could not read English or French, could better understand legal proceedings that were under French control. However, such redundancy only adds to the length of 21st century legal documents.

Most pairs can be reduced to the most common term in the pair—unless, for example, a particular legal document is known by the redundant term, such as a ***cease and desist order***.

Strategy 7

Use the space at ends of lines.

In a page format with ragged-right justification, the blank spaces at the ends of lines vary. Some lines end at the right margin and others, further from the right margin. For example, in Table 9, the second line ends closer to the right margin than does the first line.

You can fill in text, in the space at the ends of ragged-right justified lines, which can sometimes eliminate the short last line of a paragraph. Three ways to use the space are: (a) to hyphenate multi-syllabic words, (b) to rephrase sentences with URLs, and (c) to change the word order of sentences in order to position words in the space.

(a) Hyphenation. You can hyphenate a multisyllabic word so that the initial syllable(s) of the word fits in the space at the end of a line. This hyphenation reduces the number of characters on the line with the last syllable(s) of the word—a process that might ultimately shorten the last line of a paragraph. In Table 9A, the last line of the paragraph is short; it has just six characters. Through the application of Strategy 7(a), ***bankruptcy*** is hyphenated; the initial syllable ***bank-*** fills the end of the previous line with text, which ultimately eliminates the last short line in the paragraph, as shown in Table 9B.

Word-processing programs are designed so that you can activate or deactivate the hyphenation of words.[1] However, you should not adjust the program to allow global hyphenation since extensive hyphenation can lower the readability of the text. You need to apply hyphenation selectively, usually only to affect the length of a paragraph.

Authorities for legal documents submitted to courts might specify that hyphenation should not be used. In the absence of such requirements, you can manually hyphenate a few words. When this strategy is used, conventional rules of hyphenation need to be followed.[2]

(b) URLS. Some word-processing programs split a URL (a website address) across lines of text, without a hyphen. Other word-processing programs, however, automatically position the entire URL at the beginning of the next line, which can waste space, such as the wasted space at the end of line 7 in Table 10. If your word-processing program positions the entire URL at the beginning of the next line, you can revise the sentence to fit the entire URL on one line. Such revision involves: (1) reducing the

---

1. In Microsoft Word 2003, hyphenation can be accessed through the drop-down Format menu (Format > Paragraph > Line and Page Breaks).

2. For example, a word with one syllable cannot be hyphenated; a multi-syllabic word with double consonants can be hyphenated between the consonants, such as com-mittee or commit-tee; and a multi-syllabic word can be hyphenated before a consonant letter that begins a syllable, such as *hy-phenation*, *hyphe-nation*, or *hyphena-tion*. *Publication Manual of the American Psychological Association* (2009), 6th ed. Washington, D.C.: American Psychological Ass'n. Chapter 14.13.

number of words in the text before the URL so that the entire URL can fit onto the previous line or (2) rephrasing the sentence so that the URL comes earlier in the sentence and, thus, has enough space to fit on the line.[3]

In Table 10A, sentence 4 can be rephrased so that the URL fits on the previous line. The adjective phrase *altered and forged* is redundant since a forged document is an altered document. By applying Strategy 30, you can reduce *altered and forged* to *forged*.[4] In addition, *located* in sentence 4 does not add substantive information to the sentence and so it can also be eliminated under Strategy 30. With these revisions, the URL now fits on the previous line, which results in the elimination of the last line of the paragraph, as shown in Table 10B.

You can also shorten the URL by omitting *http://* or *http:// www*. However, you should not apply this strategy if the URL is a hotlink, and it should not be applied to a URL with a distinct hypertext transfer protocol, such as *https://* (an abbreviation for *hypertext transfer protocol secure*).

(c) Word-order changes. To eliminate the short last line of a paragraph, you might be able to change the order of items in a list to fill in space at end of a line. For example, in Table 11A, by reversing the order of the listed items in the sixth line— *"perished" or "decayed beyond marketability"* to *"decayed*

---

3. To reduce wasted space that may occur in a sentence with a URL, some writers rephrase the sentence and place the URL in a footnote. However, this strategy might lengthen the total length of the text due to footnote format. For example, in Word 2003, footnotes at the bottom of a page are preceded by a blank line and also a line with underscoring.

4. However, an altered document is not necessarily a forged document. If the document was forged and altered in ways that would not be considered forged, then *altered and forged* should be initially phrased *forged and otherwise altered*. Thus, *altered and forged* can be taken as redundant and can be reduced to *forged*.

beyond marketability" or "perished")—the term *"decayed"* (at eight characters) now fits into the end of line 5. As a result, the short last line is eliminated, as shown in Table 11B. Note, however, that this strategy cannot be applied to lists with items constrained to a particular order, such as lists with items in chronological order (see Strategy 11).

Table 9. Selective Hyphenation to Fill Line Space and to Shorten Paragraphs.

A. Original Text. From Doc. 8. Total line count: 9, Total word count: 111, Total character count: 740

[1]Accordingly, the Commission seeks an Order from this Court temporarily (pending a preliminary injunction hearing): (1) appointing a receiver for the assets of BMIS; (2) freezing the assets of Madoff and BMIS (except allowing the receiver to use funds to operate BMIS); (3) enjoining Madoff and BMIS from future violations of the federal securities laws; (4) permitting expedited discovery; (5) preventing the destruction of documents by Madoff and BMIS; (6) requiring verified accountings from Madoff and BMIS; and (7) enjoining BMIS and its affiliates from filing for bankruptcy protection—and enjoining anyone from seeking an involuntary **bankruptcy** against BMIS and its affiliates—without prior notice to the Commission and the Court.

B. Revised Text. Total line count: 8, Total word count: 111, Total character count: 742

[1]Accordingly, the Commission seeks an Order from this Court temporarily (pending a preliminary injunction hearing): (1) appointing a receiver for the assets of BMIS; (2) freezing the assets of Madoff and BMIS (except allowing the receiver to use funds to operate BMIS); (3) enjoining Madoff and BMIS from future violations of the federal securities laws; (4) permitting expedited discovery; (5) preventing the destruction of documents by Madoff and BMIS; (6) requiring verified accountings from Madoff and BMIS; and (7) enjoining BMIS and its affiliates from filing for bankruptcy protection—and enjoining anyone from seeking an involuntary **bank-ruptcy** against BMIS and its affiliates—without prior notice to the Commission and the Court.

Table 10. Rephrasing Sentences to Reposition URLs.

A. Line 7 ends with substantial space that could be more efficiently used. **B.** Sentence 4 is reduced through the application of Strategies 1 and 24, which makes room for the entire URL to fit onto the previous line, thus eliminating the last line of the paragraph.

A. Original Text. From Doc. 1 (line length modified). Total line count: 8, Total word count: 86, Total character count: 566

[1]Obama attempted to defraud Plaintiff and the American people by allowing an altered and forged Hawaii Certificate of Live Birth (COLB) to be placed on his campaign website. [2]Obama was well aware the Government-issued COLB was altered and forged as the original document was in the name of Maya Kasandra Soetoro born in 1970. [3]Maya Kassandra Soetoro, Obama's half sister, was born in Indonesia and her birth was later registered in Hawaii. [4]The ***altered and forged*** COLB is still on Obama's campaign website ***located at***
http://my.barackobama.com/page/invite/birthcert.

B. Revised Text. Total line count: 7, Total word count: 83, Total character count: 554

[1]Obama attempted to defraud Plaintiff and the American people by allowing an altered and forged Hawaii Certificate of Live Birth (COLB) to be placed on his campaign website. [2]Obama was well aware the Government-issued COLB was altered and forged as the original document was in the name of Maya Kasandra Soetoro born in 1970. [3]Maya Kassandra Soetoro, Obama's half sister, was born in Indonesia and her birth was later registered in Hawaii. [4]The ***forged*** COLB is still on Obama's campaign website ***at*** http://my.barackobama.com/page/invite/birthcert.

Table 11. Rearranging Items in a List to Use Space More Efficiently.

A. Original Text. From Doc. 10. Total line count: 9, Total word count: 116, Total character count: 783

[1]At the close of the plaintiffs' case-in-chief, the defendants moved for judgment as a matter of law on all of the pending claims. [2]The district court granted the motion only with respect to the plaintiffs' claim under the False Disparagement of Perishable Food Products Act. [3]The district court rested its decision on several bases. [4]First, the district court questioned the applicability of the statute to live "fed cattle." [5]Second, the court disputed whether the plaintiffs' cattle *"perished" or "decayed beyond marketability"* as required for statutory protection." [6]Alternatively, the district court ruled that the case was not cognizable under the Act because insufficient proof had been offered tending to show the defendants had knowingly disseminated false information.

B. Revised Text. Total line count: 8, Total word count: 116, Total character count: 780

[1]At the close of the plaintiffs' case-in-chief, the defendants moved for judgment as a matter of law on all of the pending claims. [2]The district court granted the motion only with respect to the plaintiffs' claim under the False Disparagement of Perishable Food Products Act. [3]The district court rested its decision on several bases. [4]First, the district court questioned the applicability of the statute to live "fed cattle." [5]Second, the court disputed whether the plaintiffs' cattle *"decayed beyond marketability" or "perished"* as required for statutory protection." [6]Alternatively, the district court ruled that the case was not cognizable under the Act because insufficient proof had been offered tending to show the defendants had knowingly disseminated false information.

Strategy 8

Shorten expressions of purpose.

The phrase *in order to + verb*[1] conveys the meaning of "higher purpose" or "ultimate purpose," and under certain conditions, *in order to* can be rephrased more concisely as *to + verb*. The *in order* can be eliminated when: (1) the sentence has no other *to + verb*, such as in Example 8 or (2) *in order* begins a sentence, such as in Example 9. However, when *in order* is needed for clarity, *in order to* cannot be omitted, such as in Example 10, where *in order to* is the higher-level purpose of *avoiding*.

To evaluate whether *in order* can be eliminated from sentences to save space, but not at the expense of clarity, you can use the **Find** function to locate every sentence with *in order* and to evaluate the sentence in which it occurs.

---

1. A similar expression of purpose is *in order for + noun*.

Example 8

In 1994, Congress passed the Jacob Wetterling Crimes Against Children and Sexually Violent Offender Registration Act ("the Wetterling Act") ~~in order~~ *to promote* the adoption of sex offender registration laws by all states.

From Doc. 14. Total word count before editing: 33, Total character count before editing: 221, Total word count after editing: 31, Total character count after editing: 219

Example 9

~~In order~~ *To fund* their conspiracy, McVeigh and Nichols robbed a gun dealer in Arkansas in November of 1994.

From Doc. 13. Total word count before editing: 19, Total character count before editing: 106, Total word count after editing: 29, Total character count after editing: 98

Example 10

[1]Thus, *in order to avoid* this plain language interpretation, Defendants ask the Court *to find* an ambiguity in an otherwise unambiguous clause of the Constitution. [2]The Court need not do so.

From Doc. 7. Total word count: 31, Total character count: 189

Strategy 9

Use numerals for cardinal numbers greater than one.

Authorities in legal writing agree that cardinal numbers[1] that begin sentences need to be spelled out. However, they do not agree on how to handle numbers within sentences. For instance, *The Blue Book*[2] prescribes that numbers 0 through 99 should be spelled out in sentences and footnotes, with certain exceptions, such as numbers that include a decimal point (e.g., *3.9*) and large round numbers (e.g., *3 thousand*). However, other writing authorities, such as the *APA Style Manual*, prescribe that numbers 0 to 10, when not beginning sentences, should be spelled out and that numerals should be used for numbers 10 and higher.

For legal documents that are not constrained by legal-writing authorities, you need to decide how you will indicate

---

1. Examples of cardinal numbers are 1, 4, and 11. Examples of ordinal numbers are 1st, 4th, and 11th.

2. *The Bluebook: A Uniform System of Citation* R.6.2 at page 73 (Columbia Law Review Ass'n et al. eds., 18th ed. 2005).

numbers within sentences, and then you need to present the numbers consistently throughout the legal document, in the style you choose.

Here are some guidelines: You may have noticed that in this handbook, cardinal numbers in the text are written out as words, not in numerals. This style follows prescriptions in the *Chicago Style Manual*, the style guide that most published books follow: it requires that numbers under 10 be spelled out. Here are some guidelines if you are not following a specific writing or legal-writing authority with rules governing numbers:

(a) Spell out numbers that start sentences and the number one.

(b) Combine words and numerals for large, rounded numbers, such as *3 million*.

(c) Use numerals for numbers with measurement units, such as *4 years*, *3.5 cm*, *2.2 kg*, and *1-day trip*.

(d) For two consecutive numbers, where the first is a count of the number of items, the first is spelled out, and the second is in a numeral, such as *four, 4-cylinder autos*.

(e) Use numerals for *all* other numbers greater than one, unless a problem in clarity could result.

(f) Avoid using both words and numerals for the same number, such as in Table 4A and 4B. In Table 4C, the words are eliminated, resulting in a savings of 5 words.

Example 11A is a sentence from an opinion written by a federal judge. Reflecting standard practices in *The Blue Book*, *Six hundred* is in words because the number begins a sentence, *450* and *182* are in numerals because they are greater than 99, and *sixteen* and *six* are spelled out because they are less than 99. Example 11B uses the guidelines in this strategy, which results in a savings of seven characters.

The text in Example 11B can be revised and shortened even more, to avoid *Six hundred* opening the sentence. This revision is illustrated in Example 11C, which shows a savings of 16 characters over Example 11A. Further, if the redundancy *the course of* is omitted (Strategy 30), leaving *over 6 weeks*, additional savings are realized, as shown in Example 11D.

Example 11

A. [1]Jury selection began November 12, 1997. [2]*Six hundred* veniremen were summoned, and *450* questionnaires were filled out. [3]Voir dire of *182* prospective jurors took *sixteen* days over the course of *six* weeks.

From Doc. 12. Total word count: 31, Total character count: 164

B. [1]Jury selection began November 12, 1997. [2]*Six hundred* veniremen were summoned, and *450* questionnaires were filled out. [3]Voir dire of *182* prospective jurors took *16* days over the course of *6* weeks.

Total word count: 31, Total character count: 157

C. [1]On November 12, 1997, *600* veniremen were summoned for jury selection, and *450* questionnaires were filled out. [2]Voir dire of *182* prospective jurors took *16* days over the course of *6* weeks.

Total word count: 31, Total character count: 183

D. [1]On November 12, 1997, *600* veniremen were summoned for jury selection, and *450* questionnaires were filled out. [2]Voir dire of *182* prospective jurors took *16* days *over 6 weeks*.

Total word count: 29, Total character count: 175

A fast way to check a document for consistent use of numbers in words or numerals is to use the find function for numbers 2 through 9. For example, in the find field, you type in the word *two* and evaluate each hit. If the located word does not begin a sentence, you replace *two* with *2* (if you are following the guidelines suggested in this handbook). Then you type the word *three* in the find field, and repeat the process. A global replacement of a numeral for a word (e.g., *4* for *four*) is not recommended since a numeral might be located at the beginning of a sentence, in which case the number needs to be spelled out, or an unusual vocabulary item could be inadvertently created, such as *4teen*. Also, for those sentences that you find beginning with numbers, you can evaluate them to see if you can rephrase by placing the numbers later in the sentence so that a numeral can be used.

Strategy 10

Punctuate and hyphenate conservatively.

The punctuation, hyphenation, and spacing that you use in abbreviations and compound nouns can affect the total word count and the length of a paragraph. The preferred practices for many standard legal terms—such as court names and cases—can be found in legal authorities.[1] In general, however, when creating an abbreviation or using compound adjectives, you need to use conservative punctuation, hyphenation, and spacing consistently throughout the legal document.

(a) Spaces in abbreviations. Typically in word-processing programs, periods in an abbreviation do not increase the word count, but spaces in an abbreviation do. For example, Microsoft Word 2003 calculates ***Ph.D.*** as one word and ***Ph. D.*** as two words.

(b) Hyphens in compound adjectives. Hyphens in compound adjectives (the punctuation preferred by writing authorities)

---

1. *Id.* R.6.1, page 72

reduce the total word count. Microsoft Word 2003 calculates the compound adjective *known-alcoholic* in Example 12A as one word, but *known alcoholic* in Example 12B as two words.

(c) Spaces with dashes. The presence or absence of spaces before and after dashes does not usually affect total word count, but spaces do increase the number of characters. The total word count in Example 12A, where spaces accompany the em dashes, is the same as in Example 12B, in which no spaces accompany the em dashes.

Example 12
A. Although the supertanker was freshly loaded with 53 million gallons of crude oil, Exxon's *known-alcoholic* captain — the only officer aboard licensed to navigate through the difficult parts of Prince William Sound — was drunk and left his post.
From Doc. 5. Total word count: 37, Total character count: 243

B. Although the supertanker was freshly loaded with 53 million gallons of crude oil, Exxon's *known alcoholic* captain—the only officer aboard licensed to navigate through the difficult parts of Prince William Sound—was drunk and left his post.
Total word count: 38, Total character count: 239

Chapter 3

Revising Lists, Phrases, and Sentences

Strategy 11. Change vertical lists into horizontal lists.

Strategy 12. Create a list from closely related information.

Strategy 13. Shorten lead-ins to lists.

Strategy 14. Revise an itemized list into an unitemized list.

Strategy 15. Reduce excessive parallelism.

Strategy 16. Change adjective clauses into adjective phrases.

Strategy 17. Reduce adjectival "*of* prepositional phrases" to adjectives.

Strategy 18. Change passive phrasing into active phrasing in subordinate grammatical units.

Strategy 19. Rephrase double negatives.

Strategy 20. Shorten wordy sentence openers.

Strategy 21. Use gapping sentence structure.

Strategy 22. Reduce emphatic phrasing and punctuation.

Strategy 23. Reduce strings of prepositional phrases.

Strategy 24. Consider omitting the optional *that*.

Strategy 11

Change vertical lists into horizontal lists.

Lists are common in both legal and non-legal writing. Although common, they can be complex to compose concisely and with the appropriate grammar and layout. Listed items can be deliberately arranged, for example, in chronological order, from most to least important, or from largest to smallest. They can also be presented in no particular order, if no order is needed to make a point.

A list can be oriented horizontally or vertically. In a *horizontal list*, each item follows on the same line as the previous item in the list, and in a *vertical list*, each item follows on the next line. Whether in a horizontal or vertical orientation, the items in a list need to be in parallel grammar (see Strategy 15).

Due to white space that frames a vertical list, the vertical list is visually more salient than is a horizontal list; thus, the vertical list is useful for emphasizing information. If you use a vertical list, its content should warrant the extra attention from the reader that the vertical orientation generates. Because a vertical list grabs the reader's attention more than does a horizontal list, only one vertical list should be used in a paragraph, to avoid sets of information vying for the reader's attention. Unlike other text-shortening strategies, a selected few vertical lists can be retained for emphasis, if you have the space.

However, to save space, you can orient all lists horizontally. Table 12A shows a paragraph with a vertical, bulleted list; in Table 12B, the list is horizontal, for a savings of six lines. In Table 12C, the horizontal list is presented with alpha itemization, which makes each item easier to locate.[1] A numeric itemization is useful to indicate items deliberately arranged in a particular order, such as in chronological order.

Sometimes lists end too soon. The information following the last item in a list might be more effectively presented as an item in the list, which can shorten the text. Table 13A gives a paragraph with a list of three items. However, the list should be comprised of four items: the fourth item is in sentence 2. As shown in Table 13B, integrating sentence 2 into the list as item 4 reduces the text by 18 words, assuming some of the detail in sentence 2 is unnecessary (see Strategy 35).

One way to modify a vertical list into a horizontal orientation is to reformat it into two columns, which can save space. This revision, illustrated in Tables 14A and 14B, works best when the listed items are short.

---

1. Alpha itemization is also used to mark items in a subordinate list.

Table 12. Lists in Vertical and Horizontal Orientation.

A. The information in the bulleted vertical list corresponds to the information in sentences 3, 4, and 5 in **B**. **C.** The list corresponds to the list in **B**, except that the items have alpha itemization. **D.** Discussed in Strategy 12: The list combines the information from sentences 4–6. Original text—and the longest text—is in **B**. From Doc. 9.

A. Text with a Vertical List. Total line count: 21, Total word count: 200, Total character count: 1263

4. [1]Specifically, as set forth in the Complaint and supporting sworn statement, BMIS is a broker-dealer registered with the Commission and controlled by Madoff. [2]Madoff, through BMIS, also conducts an investment advisory business that is separate from BMIS' proprietary trading and market-making activities. [3]On or about December 10, 2008, Madoff told two senior employees of BMIS that:

- his investment advisory business was a fraud
- his investment advisory business was "finished"
- Madoff had "absolutely nothing"
- his investment advisory business was "all one big lie"
- his investment advisory business was a "Ponzi Scheme"
- Madoff estimated the losses from this fraud to be at least $50 billion
- before surrendering to authorities in one week, Madoff planned to use the approximately $200 million he had left to make payments to selected employees, family, and friends.

[4]On December 11, 2008, Madoff confessed to F.B.I. agent Theodore Cacioppi that there was "no innocent explanation." [5]Madoff explained that he had traded and lost money for institutional clients, that it was his fault, and that he had "paid investors with money that wasn't there." [6]Madoff further said that he was "broke" and "insolvent" and that he expected to go to jail.

B. Text with a Horizontal List. Total line count: 15, Total word count: 209, Total character count: 1299

4. [1]Specifically, as set forth in the Complaint and supporting sworn statement, BMIS is a broker-dealer registered with the Commission and controlled by Madoff. [2]Madoff, through BMIS, also conducts an investment advisory business that is separate from BMIS' proprietary trading and market-making activities. [3]On or about December 10, 2008, Madoff told two senior employees of BMIS that his investment advisory business was a fraud, that it was "finished," that Madoff had "absolutely nothing," that it was "all one big lie," and that it was a "Ponzi Scheme" [4]In that same conversation, Madoff told the two senior employees that he estimated the losses from this fraud to be at least $50 billion. [5]Madoff also told the two senior employees that before surrendering to authorities in one week, he planned to use the approximately $200 million he had left to make payments to certain selected employees, family, and friends. [6]On December 11, 2008, Madoff confessed to F.B.I. agent Theodore Cacioppi that there was "no innocent explanation." [7]Madoff explained that he had traded and lost money for institutional clients, that it was his fault, and that he had "paid investors with money that wasn't there." [8]Madoff further said that he was "broke" and "insolvent" and that he expected to go to jail.

C. Revised Text with a Horizontal List and Alpha Itemization. Total line count: 14, Total word count: 201, Total character count: 1225

4. [1]Specifically, as set forth in the Complaint and supporting sworn statement, BMIS is a broker-dealer registered with the Commission and controlled by Madoff. [2]Madoff, through BMIS, also conducts an investment advisory business that is separate from BMIS' proprietary trading and market-making activities. [3]On or about December 10, 2008, Madoff told two senior employees of BMIS that: *(a)* his investment advisory business was a fraud, *(b)* it was "finished," *(c)* Madoff had "absolutely nothing," *(d)* it was "all one big lie," *(e)* it was a "Ponzi Scheme," *(f)* he estimated the losses from this fraud to be at least $50 billion, and *(g)* he planned to surrender to authorities in one week, but that, before he did that, he planned to use the approximately $200 million he had left to make payments to certain selected employees, family, and friends. [4]On December 11, 2008, Madoff confessed to F.B.I. agent Theodore Cacioppi that there was "no innocent explanation." [5]Madoff explained that he had traded and lost money for institutional clients, that it was his fault, and that he had "paid investors with money that wasn't there." [6]Madoff further said that he was "broke" and "insolvent" and that he expected to go to jail.

D. Another Revised Text with a Second Horizontal List. Total line count: 13, Total word count: 190, Total character count: 1169

4. [1]Specifically, as set forth in the Complaint and supporting sworn statement, BMIS is a broker-dealer registered with the Commission and controlled by Madoff. [2]Madoff, through BMIS, also conducts an investment advisory business that is separate from BMIS' proprietary trading and market-making activities. [3]On or about December 10, 2008, Madoff told two senior employees of BMIS that: *(a)* his investment advisory business was a fraud, *(b)* it was "finished," *(c)* Madoff had "absolutely nothing," *(d)* it was "all one big lie," *(e)* it was a "Ponzi Scheme," *(f)* he estimated the losses from this fraud to be at least $50 billion, and *(g)* he planned to surrender to authorities in one week, but that, before he did that, he planned to use the approximately $200 million he had left to make payments to certain selected employees, family, and friends.

[4]On December 11, 2008, Madoff confessed to F.B.I. agent Theodore Cacioppi that: Madoff had "no innocent explanation," he had traded and lost money for institutional clients, it was his fault, he had "paid investors with money that wasn't there," he was "broke" and "insolvent," and he expected to go to jail.

Table 13. Reduction of a Paragraph by Integrating a Sentence into an Existing List.

A. Original Text. From Doc. 13. Total line count: 7, Total word count: 82, Total character count: 484

¹McVeigh told the Fortiers that he chose the Murrah Building as the target because he believed that (1) the orders for the attack at Waco emanated from the building, (2) the building housed people involved in the Waco raid, **and (3)** the building's U-shape and glass front made it an easy target. ²On a later trip through Oklahoma City, McVeigh showed Michael Fortier the Murrah Building, asking Fortier whether he thought a twenty-foot rental truck would fit in front of the building.

B. Revised Text. Total line count: 5, Total word count: 64, Total character count: 360

¹McVeigh told the Fortiers that he chose the Murrah Building as the target because he believed that (1) the orders for the attack at Waco emanated from the building, (2) the building housed people involved in the Waco raid, (3) the building's U-shape and glass front made it an easy target, **and (4)** a twenty-foot rental truck would fit in front of the building.

Table 14. A Two-Column Vertical List.

List was originally formatted horizontally (from Doc. 11); line length has been adjusted from the original.

A. Text with a bulleted vertical list. Total line count: 13, Total word count: 92, Total character count: 606

[1]During the search, I observed containers containing powders labeled accordingly:

- "KC103" (potassium chlorate)
- "NaC103" (sodium chlorate)
- "Sugar"
- "Zinc"
- "Aluminum"
- "Lead"
- "Silver Oxide"

[2]Necessary ingredients in the preparation of explosives include an oxidizer and a fuel. Sugar, zinc, aluminum, lead, and silver oxide all can serve as fuels, and potassium chlorate or sodium chlorate can be oxidizers. [3]For example, potassium chlorate can be combined with either aluminum or sugar to create an explosive material. [4]Similarly, sodium chlorate can be combined with aluminum to create an explosive.

B. Revised Text. Total line count: 10, Total word count: 92, Total character count: 681

[1]During the search, I observed containers containing powders labeled accordingly:

- "KC103" (potassium chlorate)
- "NaC103" (sodium chlorate)
- "Sugar"
- "Zinc"
- "Aluminum"
- "Lead"
- "Silver Oxide"

[2]Necessary ingredients in the preparation of explosives include an oxidizer and a fuel. Sugar, zinc, aluminum, lead, and silver oxide all can serve as fuels, and potassium chlorate or sodium chlorate can be oxidizers. [3]For example, potassium chlorate can be combined with either aluminum or sugar to create an explosive material. [4]Similarly, sodium chlorate can be combined with aluminum to create an explosive.

Strategy 12

Create a list from closely related information.

You might have drafted a paragraph without a list. You can examine the paragraph to see if the information can be reformatted into a list, which can shorten the text and help readers see relationships among pieces of information.

You can create a list by: (a) identifying information that is repeated within the same sentence or across sentences, (b) creating a lead-in to a list, using the repeated information, and (c) identifying information as items in the list from the remaining information in the sentence(s). For example, the last three sentences in Table 12A have information that is similar: information that Madoff provided to the FBI agent. To save space, that information can be presented as a separate list, in its own paragraph, as shown in Table 12D. The lead-in identifies what the list is about, and the listed items identify the actual information that Madoff provided. The creation of this second list reduces the text by one line over the version in Table 12C.

For another example, sentences 3 and 4 in Table 15A repeat the information *the district court found that*. In Table 15B, this repeated information is transformed into the lead-in, and the remaining information comprises the items in the list. The creation of this list results in the elimination of the short last line of the paragraph and a reduction of four words.

Sentence 2 in Table 15A also has a list, but it is buried. Making the list explicit will shorten the text. The first item is introduced with *on the basis that* and the second, with *because*. Assuming that *on the basis that* and *because* are synonyms—and hence can be considered repeated information—you can change *on the basis that* to its shorter synonym *because* (Strategy 1), and the remaining information comprises the items in the list. The creation of this list further shortens the paragraph by one line and four words (see Table 15C).

Table 15. Creation of an Itemized List.

A. Original Text. From Doc. 3. Total line count: 16, Total word count: 181, Total character count: 1192

[1]In 1999, the United States ("Government") filed a civil complaint seeking to revoke Petitioner's citizenship. [2]On February 21, 2002, the district court revoked Petitioner's naturalized U.S. citizenship *on the basis that* he procured his citizenship by concealing and misrepresenting his SS guard service at Nazi-operated concentration camps and an extermination center during World War II and *because* his assistance in Nazi persecution rendered him ineligible to enter the United States. *United Sates v. Demjanjuk*, 2002 WL 544622 (N.D. Ohio Feb. 21, 2002) (unpublished). [3]In particular, *the district court found that Petitioner* "contributed to the process by which thousands of Jews were murdered by asphyxiation with carbon monoxide" in the gas chambers in the Sobibor extermination center in Nazi-occupied Poland. *Demjanjuk*, 202 WL 544622 at *21. [4]*The district court also found that he* assisted in Nazi persecution by serving as an armed guard at the Majdanek and Flossenburg concentration camps. *Id.* at *27. [5]On April 30, 2004, this Court affirmed the revocation of Petitioner's U.S. citizenship. *United States v. Demjanjuk*, 367 F.3d 623 (6th Cir.), *cert. denied*, 543 U.S. 970 (2004).

B. Revised Text with an Itemized List. Total line count: 15, Total word count: 177, Total character count: 1167

[1]In 1999, the United States ("Government") filed a civil complaint seeking to revoke Petitioner's citizenship. [2]On February 21, 2002, the district court revoked Petitioner's naturalized U.S. citizenship *on the basis that* he procured his citizenship by concealing and misrepresenting his SS guard service at Nazi-operated concentration camps and an extermination center during World War II and *because* his assistance in Nazi persecution rendered him ineligible to enter the United States. *United Sates v. Demjanjuk*, 2002 WL 544622 (N.D. Ohio Feb. 21, 2002) (unpublished). [3]In particular, *the district court found that Petitioner: (1)* "contributed to the process by which thousands of Jews were murdered by asphyxiation with carbon monoxide" in the gas chambers in the Sobibor extermination center in Nazi-occupied Poland. *Demjanjuk*, 202 WL 544622 at *21; and *(2)* assisted in Nazi persecution by serving as an armed guard at the Majdanek and Flossenburg concentration camps. *Id.* at *27. [4]On April 30, 2004, this Court affirmed the revocation of Petitioner's U.S. citizenship. *United States v. Demjanjuk*, 367 F.3d 623 (6th Cir.), *cert. denied*, 543 U.S. 970 (2004).

C. Revised Text with an Unitemized List. Total line count: 14, Total word count: 173, Total character count: 1155

[1]In 1999, the United States ("Government") filed a civil complaint seeking to revoke Petitioner's citizenship. [2]On February 21, 2002, the district court revoked Petitioner's naturalized U.S. citizenship *because* he procured his citizenship by concealing and misrepresenting his SS guard service at Nazi-operated concentration camps and an extermination center during World War II *and because* his assistance in Nazi persecution rendered him ineligible to enter the United States. *United Sates v. Demjanjuk*, 2002 WL 544622 (N.D. Ohio Feb. 21, 2002) (unpublished). [3]In particular, *the district court found that Petitioner: (1)* "contributed to the process by which thousands of Jews were murdered by asphyxiation with carbon monoxide" in the gas chambers in the Sobibor extermination center in Nazi-occupied Poland. *Demjanjuk*, 202 WL 544622 at *21; and *(2)* assisted in Nazi persecution by serving as an armed guard at the Majdanek and Flossenburg concentration camps. *Id.* at *27. [4]On April 30, 2004, this Court affirmed the revocation of Petitioner's U.S. citizenship. *United States v. Demjanjuk*, 367 F.3d 623 (6th Cir.), *cert. denied*, 543 U.S. 970 (2004).

Shorten lead-ins to lists.

The lead-in to a list is sometimes too wordy, as illustrated in Table 16A. Table 16A has two lists[1]: one in sentence 7 and one in sentence 8. Both lists use lead-ins that are phrased with ***the following***. However, this phrase is not needed in these instances because the lists follow their lead-ins. Omitting ***the following*** eliminates the last short line and reduces the word count by four, as shown in Table 16B.

In Table 16A, the lead-ins to the lists can be further shortened. In Table 16A, the phrase ***include, but not limited to*** (or the phrase ***include without limitation***) indicates that you are leaving the list open for other items—items that may be members of other types or categories not represented by the listed items. If such open-ended phrasing is not needed for your legal case, the phrase ***but are not limited to*** can be omitted. Table 16C shows the phrase ***but are not limited to*** omitted from the lead-in in sentence 6—an omission that further reduces the total word count from the original 219 to 210.

---

1. Table 16A has more than two lists, but only two are discussed here.

Table 16. Shortening Lead-Ins to Lists.

A. Original Text. From Doc. 15. Total line count: 16, Total word count: 219, Total character count: 1370

[1]After the crash, the Emergency Locator Transmitter (ELT) transmitted a message via satellite which the USCG Command Center received. [2]The ELT provided the Global Positioning Satellite Coordinates for the downed aircraft. [3]The USCG HH65 rescue helicopter arrived at the scene, as did the Santa Rosa County Sheriff's Office (SRCSO) Water Response Unit. [4]The HH65 rescue helicopter crew reported that there appeared to be no one inside the wrecked aircraft. [5]This fact was later confirmed by Sergeant (Sgt.) Ricky Perritt of the SRCSO Special Operations Unit. [6]A subsequent inspection of the aircraft by Sgt. Perritt revealed that the front windshields of the aircraft were still intact after the crash. [7]Sgt. Perritt and members of the Special Operations Unit also recovered several items of evidence which ***include, but are not limited to, the following***: a fifty (50) state road map book, of which the states Alabama and Florida were ripped out; a book containing the campsites of America, of which the states Alabama and Florida were also ripped from the book. [8]On the back of one of the books was what appeared to be a list containing bullet summary points which ***included the following***: "cracked wind shield, window imploded, bleeding profusely" or words to that effect. [9]Also located in the plane were Meals Ready to Eat (MREs) and other survival paraphernalia.

B. Revised Text, with a Shortened Lead-In to a List. Total line count: 15, Total word count: 215, Total character count: 1340

[1]After the crash, the Emergency Locator Transmitter (ELT) transmitted a message via satellite which the USCG Command Center received. [2]The ELT provided the Global Positioning Satellite Coordinates for the downed aircraft. [3]The USCG HH65 rescue helicopter arrived at the scene, as did the Santa Rosa County Sheriff's Office (SRCSO) Water Response Unit. [4]The HH65 rescue helicopter crew reported that there appeared to be no one inside the wrecked aircraft. This fact was later confirmed by Sergeant (Sgt.) Ricky Perritt of the SRCSO Special Operations Unit. [5]A subsequent inspection of the aircraft by Sgt. Perritt revealed that the front windshields of the aircraft were still intact after the crash. [6]Sgt. Perritt and members of the Special Operations Unit also recovered several items of evidence which *included, but are not limited to*: a fifty (50) state road map book, of which the states Alabama and Florida were ripped out; a book containing the campsites of America, of which the states Alabama and Florida were also ripped from the book. [7]On the back of one of the books was what appeared to be a list containing bullet summary points which included: "cracked wind shield, window imploded, bleeding profusely" or words to that effect. [8]Also located in the plane were Meals Ready to Eat (MREs) and other survival paraphernalia.

C. Revised Text, with the Lead-In Further Reduced. Total line count: 15, Total word count: 210, Total character count: 1316

[1]After the crash, the Emergency Locator Transmitter (ELT) transmitted a message via satellite which the USCG Command Center received. [2]The ELT provided the Global Positioning Satellite Coordinates for the downed aircraft. [3]The USCG HH65 rescue helicopter arrived at the scene, as did the Santa Rosa County Sheriff's Office (SRCSO) Water Response Unit. [4]The HH65 rescue helicopter crew reported that there appeared to be no one inside the wrecked aircraft. This fact was later confirmed by Sergeant (Sgt.) Ricky Perritt of the SRCSO Special Operations Unit. [5]A subsequent inspection of the aircraft by Sgt. Perritt revealed that the front windshields of the aircraft were still intact after the crash. [6]Sgt. Perritt and members of the Special Operations Unit also recovered several items of evidence which **included**: a fifty (50) state road map book, of which the states Alabama and Florida were ripped out; a book containing the campsites of America, of which the states Alabama and Florida were also ripped from the book. [7]On the back of one of the books was what appeared to be a list containing bullet summary points which **included**: "cracked wind shield, window imploded, bleeding profusely" or words to that effect. [8]Also located in the plane were Meals Ready to Eat (MREs) and other survival paraphernalia.

Strategy 14

Revise an itemized list into an unitemized list.

Items in a list can be serialized through numerical (Table 13A), bulleted (Table 12A), or alpha itemization (Table 12C). Items in a list can also be presented without itemization (Table 12D, second paragraph). An unitemized list is characterized by: (a) a series of items, (b) punctuation separating each item from the other, (c) a coordinating conjunction, such as *and*, *or*, *yet*, or *but* that precedes the last item, and (d) parallel grammar across the items in the list (Strategy 15).

The shortest format is the unitemized list since no characters are used to mark where each item in the list begins. To shorten the text, you can omit the itemization, unless it is needed for clarity or emphasis.

Strategy 15

Reduce excessive parallelism.

Parallelism is the repetition of grammar across items in a list to help readers associate the listed items with each other. Parallelism is a mark of educated prose. Regardless of the type of legal document and the audience for whom the legal document is intended, parallelism is needed across all items in a list. However, the extent of parallelism can vary, depending on clarity and on the degree of emphasis that you want to confer on particular information.

The greater the parallelism, the greater the emphasis. In Example 13, sentence 3 gives a list with emphatic parallelism. The list *an unusual case and an unusual defendant* cannot be reduced to *an unusual case and defendant* without a loss in emphasis. Also, without the repetition of *unusual*, it is not clear whether *unusual* modifies both *case* and *defendant*, or only *case*. Further, without the repetition of *unusual*, the contrast between *unusual* in sentence 3 and *ordinary* in sentence 2 is lost.

Example 13

[1]Your Honor, I recognize that you are an unusually compassionate judge, and that you sincerely believe yourself to be acting in my best interest in seeking to prevent me from representing myself. [2]In an ordinary case your course would be the most compassionate one, and the one most likely to preserve the defendant's life. [3]But I beg you to consider that you are dealing *with an unusual case and an unusual defendant* and that preventing me from representing myself is not the most compassionate course or the one most likely to preserve my life.

From Doc. 12.

In contrast to emphatic parallelism, excessive parallelism can be reduced to save space. The term *excessive parallelism* refers to parallelism that is not needed for grammatical correctness, clarity, or emphasis. In other words, excessive parallelism is the unnecessary repetition of grammatical forms and words. By reducing excessive parallelism across items in a list, you can shorten the total word count and possibly the number of lines in a paragraph.

For example, in Table 17A, sentence 3 has an unitemized list of two items, which identifies the recipients of payments: *to commercial fishermen* and *to women*. The second *to* (at the end of line 6) can be eliminated, as shown in Table 17B. The list is still parallel because *commercial fishermen* and *women* are both nouns, and they both are part of the phrase beginning with *to*. In addition to the unitemized list, sentence 3 also has an itemized list. Each item in the list begins with the preposition *for*. By eliminating *for* from each item and placing *for* into the lead-in, as shown in Table 17B, the last short line of the paragraph is eliminated and the total word count is reduced.

Table 17. Reduction of Excessive Parallelism.

Text in A is identical to the original except that *to* has been added at the end of line 6.

A. Original Text. From Doc. 5. Total line count: 22, Total word count: 164, Total character count: 1099

[1]Faced with the prospect of thousands of additional individual claims, Exxon set up a program under which it agreed to pay claims resulting from the spill. [2]These settlements, however, did not fully compensate the plaintiffs for their losses. [3]In particular, Exxon's payments *to* commercial fishermen and *to* women under these agreements compensated them for losses due to cancelled fisheries in 1989 but did not compensate them (1) *for* the diminished prices of fish in 1989, (2) *for* the losses associated with the post-1989 harvests, or (3) *for* the decline in the value of fishing permits and vessels. [4]This litigation—which involves the economic harms to 32,677 commercial fishermen, related individuals and businesses, private landowners, Native Alaskans, municipalities, and others—brought recovery for some, but not all, of the additional economic harm suffered by the plaintiffs. [5]These plaintiffs, however, never recovered for their significant non-economic harm such as the "severe depression, post-traumatic stress disorder, [and] generalized anxiety disorder" that they suffered. Pet. App. 123a.

B. Revised Text. Total line count: 21, Total word count: 161, Total character count: 1096

[1]Faced with the prospect of thousands of additional individual claims, Exxon set up a program under which it agreed to pay claims resulting from the spill. [2]These settlements, however, did not fully compensate the plaintiffs for their losses. [3]In particular, Exxon's payments *to* commercial fishermen and women under these agreements compensated them for losses due to cancelled fisheries in 1989 but did not compensate them *for* (1) the diminished prices of fish in 1989, (2) the losses associated with the post-1989 harvests, or (3) the decline in the value of fishing permits and vessels. [4]This litigation—which involves the economic harms to 32,677 commercial fishermen, related individuals and businesses, private landowners, Native Alaskans, municipalities, and others—brought recovery for some, but not all, of the additional economic harm suffered by the plaintiffs. [5]These plaintiffs, however, never recovered for their significant non-economic harm such as the "severe depression, post-traumatic stress disorder, [and] generalized anxiety disorder" that they suffered. Pet. App. 123a.

Strategy 16

Change adjective clauses into adjective phrases.

An adjective clause is a subordinate clause that modifies the preceding noun. As a clause, an adjective clause has both a subject and a verb, and is introduced by a relative pronoun, such as **who**, **that**, or **which**. Examples 14A, 15A, 16A, and 17A have adjective clauses (bold italics) that modify preceding nouns (underscored).

Example 14

A. As the Government notes, the Adam Walsh Act was enacted with <u>a commendable goal</u>, **which is to protect the public from sex offenders**.

Total word count: 23, Total character count: 131

B. As the Government notes, the Adam Walsh Act was enacted with <u>a commendable goal</u>—**to protect the public from sex offenders**.

From Doc. 14. Total word count: 21, Total character count: 123

Example 15

A. Three weeks before the taping of the "Dangerous Food" show, <u>Andrea Wishom</u>, *who is a researcher for the Oprah Winfrey Show*, conducted research and interviewed <u>individuals *who were knowledgeable about CJD and "Mad Cow Disease."*</u>

Modified, From Doc. 10. Total word count: 35, Total character count: 225

B. Three weeks before the taping of the "Dangerous Food" show, <u>Andrea Wishom</u>, *a researcher for the Oprah Winfrey Show*, conducted research and interviewed <u>individuals</u> *knowledgeable about CJD and "Mad Cow Disease."*

Total word count: 31, Total character count: 209

Example 16

A. CJD, a form of Transmissible Spongiform Encephalopathy, is <u>a fatal disease</u> *that affects the human brain.*

From Doc. 10, and sentence 2 in Table 18. Total word count: 16, Total character count: 104

B. CJD, a form of Transmissible Spongiform Encephalopathy, is <u>a fatal disease</u> *affecting the human brain.*

Total word count: 15, Total character count: 101

Example 17

A. BSE is most likely to arise when cattle are fed <u>contaminated, ruminant-derived protein supplements</u> *which are made* from rendered cattle and sheep.

From Doc. 10, and sentence 5 in Table 18. Total word count: 22, Total character count: 145

B. BSE is most likely to arise when cattle are fed <u>contaminated, ruminant-derived protein supplements</u> *made* from rendered cattle and sheep.

Total word count: 20, Total character count: 135

To save space, instead of using an entire adjective clause to modify a noun, you can change it into an adjective phrase. How you shorten an adjective clause into an adjective phrase depends on whether the adjective clause has a linking verb or an action verb.

(a) Adjective clauses with linking verbs. The adjective clauses in Examples 14A and 15A have linking verbs that equate the subject to its predicate. This type of adjective clause is shortened into a phrase by the elimination of (1) the relative pronoun and (2) its linking verb. These eliminations result in just the predicate remaining, which can be either an adjective, a noun, or an infinitive verb.

Adjective Clause with Linking Verb	Adjective Phrase
~~which is~~ *to protect the public* . . .	*to protect the public* . . . (Example 14A)
~~who is~~ *a researcher for*	*a researcher for* (Example 15A)
~~who were~~ *knowledgeable about* . . .	*knowledgeable about* . . . (Example 15A)

(b) Adjective clauses with action verbs. Some adjective clauses, such as the one in Example 16A, have action verbs, not linking verbs. An action verb can be phrased in active or passive grammar. In Example 16A, the adjective clause *that affects the human brain* uses the action verb *affects* in active grammar. In

Example 17A, the adjective clause *which are made from rendered cattle and sheep* has the action verb *are made* in passive grammar.

Adjective clauses with action verbs can be shortened by: (1) eliminating the relative pronoun and (2) retaining the participial form of the verb. In active phrasing, the participial form is *verb + ing*, and in passive phrasing, the participial form is the past participle. The *verb + ing* participial form subtly conveys the meaning of causality or consequence.

Adjective Clause with Action Verb	**Adjective Phrase**
~~that~~ *affects (+ ing) the human brain*	*affecting the human brain* (active) (Example 16)
~~which are~~ *made from . . .*	*made from . . .* (passive) (Example 17)

Similar to the reduction of adjective clauses with linking verbs, the reduction of adjective clauses with action verbs can also eliminate words and multiple characters, and possibly the last short line of a paragraph. The paragraph in Table 18A has two adjective clauses: one in sentence 2 (Example 16A) and one in sentence 6 (Example 17A). As shown in Table 18B, this strategy, applied to the last sentence, results in a reduction of two words and the elimination of the short last line of the paragraph. Application of this strategy to sentence 2 in Table 18C further reduces the paragraph by two more words.

Table 18. Reduction of Adjective Clauses to Shorten the Text.

A. Original Text. From Doc. 10. Total line count: 9, Total word count: 112, Total character count: 743

[1]In early 1996, a new variant of Creutzeld-Jakob Disease ("CJD") was diagnosed in Britain. [2]CJD, a form of Transmissible Spongiform Encephalopathy, is a fatal disease *that affects the human brain.* [3]On March 20, 1996, the British Ministry of Health announced that scientists had linked the consumption of beef infected with Bovine Spongiform Encephalopathy ("BSE") with this new CJD variant. [4]BSE, or "Mad Cow Disease," had been detected in British cattle as early as 1986. [5]Also a form of Transmissible Spongiform Encephalopathy, BSE triggers a deadly, degenerative brain condition in cattle. [6]BSE is most likely to arise when cattle are fed contaminated ruminant-derived protein supplements*, which are made* from rendered cattle and sheep.

B. Revised Text. Total line count: 8, Total word count: 110, Total character count: 732

[1]In early 1996, a new variant of Creutzeld-Jakob Disease ("CJD") was diagnosed in Britain. [2]CJD, a form of Transmissible Spongiform Encephalopathy, is a fatal disease *that affects the human brain.* [3]On March 20, 1996, the British Ministry of Health announced that scientists had linked the consumption of beef infected with Bovine Spongiform Encephalopathy ("BSE") with this new CJD variant. [4]BSE, or "Mad Cow Disease," had been detected in British cattle as early as 1986. [5]Also a form of Transmissible Spongiform Encephalopathy, BSE triggers a deadly, degenerative brain condition in cattle. [6]BSE is most likely to arise when cattle are fed contaminated ruminant-derived protein supplements *made* from rendered cattle and sheep.

C. Another Revision to the Text. Total line count: 8, Total word count: 109, Total character count: 729

[1]In early 1996, a new variant of Creutzeld-Jakob Disease ("CJD") was diagnosed in Britain. [2]CJD, a form of Transmissible Spongiform Encephalopathy, is a fatal disease *affecting* the human brain. [3]On March 20, 1996, the British Ministry of Health announced that scientists had linked the consumption of beef infected with Bovine Spongiform Encephalopathy ("BSE") with this new CJD variant. BSE, or "Mad Cow Disease," had been detected in British cattle as early as 1986. [4]Also a form of Transmissible Spongiform Encephalopathy, BSE triggers a deadly, degenerative brain condition in cattle. [5]BSE is most likely to arise when cattle are fed contaminated ruminant-derived protein supplements, *made* from rendered cattle and sheep.

Strategy 17

Reduce adjectival "*of* prepositional phrases" to adjectives.

Some prepositional phrases function as adjectives by modifying nouns, such as *of BMIS* in *the accounts of BMIS*, in sentence 3 of Table 19A. One way to shorten the text is to eliminate *of* and to use its noun as an adjective to modify the antecedent. This revision, applied to sentence 3 in Table 19A, for example, uses *BMIS* to modify *the accounts*, as shown in Table 19B, and eliminates the short last line of the paragraph.

When reducing adjectival *of* phrases to adjectives, you have a choice: you can use the possessive form of its noun (with an apostrophe and no article *the* or *a*) or the non-possessive form (without an apostrophe). For example, you can use revise *the accounts of BMIS* into *the BMIS accounts* or *BMIS' accounts*. The meaning difference may be important, depending on what you want to suggest. If you want to indicate possession, ownership, or a holding, the possessive form is more appropriate. Thus, the possessive form *BMIS' accounts* is used in sentence 3 of

Table 19A and 19B. However, if possession, ownership, or a holding is irrelevant or not an issue, and you want to only name or describe something, then the non-possessive form is more appropriate, such as ***BMIS accounts***.

Adjectival *of* **Prepositional Phrase**	**Noun** **with Adjective**
the accounts of BMIS	*the BMIS accounts*
	BMIS' accounts

Grammatical parallelism might be a factor in your choosing the possessive over the nonpossessive form of the noun, or vice versa. For example, the term ***BMIS' assets*** precedes ***the accounts of BMIS*** in sentence 3 of Table 19A. Because ***BMIS' assets*** is already in the possessive form earlier in the sentence, the possessive ***BMIS' accounts*** can be used later in the sentence for grammatical parallelism.

Whether you use the possessive or non-possessive form of a noun that was formerly in an *of* prepositional phrase, reducing the adjectival phrase can eliminate the last short line of a paragraph, such as in Table 19.

Table 19. Reduction of Possessive Prepositional Phrases.
Line length in A was modified from the original, but the paragraph was still seven lines long.

A. Original Text. From Doc. 8. Total line count: 7, Total word count: 88, Total character count: 560

[1]As described above, the Commission staff has developed significant evidence that Madoff and BMIS have committed a Ponzi-scheme of $50 billion. [2]Madoff is now seeking to distribute the remaining assets to employees, family and friends, which would be unfair to the remaining clients and creditors. [3]Thus, an immediate asset freeze is necessary to prevent further dissipation of funds from any such accounts, to permit an accounting of ***BMIS' assets***, and to sort through the tangle of anticipated competing claims to any funds remaining ***in the accounts of BMIS***.

B. Revised Text. Total line count: 6, Total word count: 86, Total character count: 554

[1]As described above, the Commission staff has developed significant evidence that Madoff and BMIS have committed a Ponzi-scheme of $50 billion. [2]Madoff is now seeking to distribute the remaining assets to employees, family and friends, which would be unfair to the remaining clients and creditors. [3]Thus, an immediate asset freeze is necessary to prevent further dissipation of funds from any such accounts, to permit an accounting of ***BMIS' assets***, and to sort through the tangle of anticipated competing claims to any funds remaining ***in BMIS' accounts***.

Change passive phrasing into active phrasing in subordinate grammatical units.

Sometimes legal and non-legal writing authorities caution against using passive grammar—possibly because courts have found statutes with passive grammar ambiguous.[1]

Passive grammar is not inherently ambiguous, but it is a concern when aiming to shorten a legal document since a sentence phrased in passive grammar can be longer in the number of words or characters than its active counterpart.

To evaluate the use or misuse of passive grammar, two important questions about content are considered. Then a brief review of passive and active grammar follows in order to clarify

---

1. For example, *see* State ex rel. Click v. Brownhill, 331 Or. 500, 509, 15 P.2d 990 (2000).

how active or passive grammar can be used to shorten the text and not impact clarity.

To evaluate whether the use of passive grammar in a sentence is appropriate, you need to answer two important questions about the content in the paragraph that you are evaluating for wordiness: *1. What is the paragraph or the series of paragraphs mainly about, and 2. Is the agent important to the discussion?*

(1) What is the paragraph mainly about? You need to identify what the paragraph is mainly about. A paragraph should only have one or two main topics in order to help readers focus on your point. Then you need to make sure that *the grammatical subjects* of most of the sentences and main clauses in the paragraph reflect the topic. By focusing on the subjects, the English language will automatically use passive or active verbs to grammatically match the verbs to their subjects. For example, in Table 20, the subjects/topics of the first two sentences are *events and evidence* and *Bundy*, respectively; those two topics are what the paragraph is mainly about. Indeed, most of the subsequent sentences in the paragraph (sentences 3, 4, 5, and 7) use *Bundy* as the subject.

Once you produce a paragraph that focuses on appropriate content for the subject, then you can address the second content question:

(2) Is the agent important to the discussion? The agent is the person or thing that is/was doing the verb action. For example, in Example 16A (sentence 3 from Table 20), the agent is Bundy; he is the person who identified himself to the officer. In Example 18A, the agent in this active sentence is *he*, referring to Bundy. In Example 18B, the agent in this passive sentence is identified in the phrase *by him*, referring to Bundy. And perhaps most importantly for the discussion here, in Example 18C, the shortest sentence among the alternatives, the agent in the passive sentence is not identified. This type of passive grammar in Example 18C, with the agent not identified with the passive verb, is called *agentless passive*.

Example 18

A. During this time *he* revealed his true identity. (active)

From Doc. 2, sentence 3 from Table 20. Total word count: 8, Total character count: 47

B. During this time the true identity was revealed *by him*. (passive)

Total word count: 10, Total character count: 55

C. During this time his true identity was revealed. (agentless passive)

Total word count: 8, Total character count: 48.

The agentless passive can be problematic: (a) if it is absolutely clear, from the text or context, who the agent is, *agentless passive* might be appropriate, but see item (c) in this paragraph, (b) if it is *not* absolutely clear who the agent is from the text or context, *agentless passive needs to be revised to include the agent in order to improve clarity*, or (c) identification of the agent may be important to the discussion or to the legal case, in which case *agentless passive needs to be revised to include the agent*. Given the nature of law and the legal arena—which deals with agents and their impact on the world according to rules of law—in many, if not most, legal documents, identification of the agent is important. Therefore, in most cases, agentless passive is problematic and needs to be revised, even though agentless passive may be the shortest phrasing. Consider Example 19, also from Table 20:

Example 19

Later **Bundy** was indicted, convicted, and sentenced to death for the Chi Omega murders.

From Doc. 2, sentence 8 from Table 20. Total word count: 14, Total character count: 86

Example 19 is an agentless passive sentence. Although the agent—in this case, the court—is not included, it is clear from the context who the agent is, since no one else may perform the verbs **indicted**, **convicted**, and **sentenced**. Since the agent (the court) is clear from the context, and the court is not the topic of discussion or necessarily important to the paragraph, the agent-less passive is appropriate. Now consider Example 20:

Example 20

A. Over the next several days Bundy was extensively interviewed **by officers from the Pensacola and Tallahassee Police Departments and the Leon County Sheriff's Office**. (passive)

From Doc. 2, sentence 4 from Table 20. Total word count: 24, Total character count: 164

B. Over the next several days Bundy was extensively interviewed. (agentless passive)

Total word count: 9, Total character count: 61

In Example 20A, the agent in this passive sentence is explicitly identified: **by officers** . . . This agent identification is appropriate since one of the paragraph topics involves **evidence**, and the officers and their identity are relevant to the quality of evidence, and the agent cannot be assumed from the context or text. Therefore, although agentless passive is much shorter in Example 20B, it is inappropriate.

Another question related to the use of passive and active in order to shorten the text is whether you can use the shorter active form instead of the longer passive form with the agent. The answer is a qualified yes. In sentences with subordination, active phrasing can be used since subordinate information conveys less important information than the main parts of the sentence. Consider sentence 4 from Table 21 and reproduced here as Example 21:

Example 21

A. Nor does the historical record provide any basis whatsoever for the conclusion *that a Member's ineligibility could be "fixed" by Congress*. (active main clause, passive subordinate clause)

Sentence 4 from Table 20. Total word count: 21, Total character count: 138

B. Nor does the historical record provide any basis whatsoever for the conclusion *that Congress could "fix" a Member's ineligibility*. (active main clause, active subordinate clause)

Total word count: 19, Total character count: 130

The subordinate clause (bold italicized) in Example 21A can be phrased in active or passive grammar. The active counterpart in Example 21B reduces the text by one word and eight characters, which is enough in Table 21B to eliminate the short last line of the paragraph.

The view here is that passive grammar does not warrant the attention it has received in legal and non-legal writing disciplines. (Ironically, however, the extent of that attention results in the need for the lengthy discussion here.) For speakers of English with native fluency who are writers of legal documents: (a) the grammatical subjects of sentences and clauses need your attention, to make sure they reflect the topic(s) of the paragraph; the verbs, in terms of their passive or active status and grammar, will take care of themselves, and (b) the agent needs your attention, to make sure you include it (in most instances).

However, to reduce the number of words in a legal document, you can use active grammar in subordinate clauses, and to reduce the number of lines in a paragraph, you might find the use of active grammar in a subordinate clause will eliminate the short last line of a paragraph.

Table 20. Passive and Active Phrasing Used to Achieve Consistent Focus.
From Doc. 2.

[1]The ***events and evidence*** leading to the investigation, trial, and conviction of Bundy are as follows: [2]On February 15, 1978, Bundy ***was arrested*** in Pensacola, Florida, after fleeing from a stop ***made by an officer whose suspicions had been aroused***. [3]At that time ***Bundy identified*** himself to the officer as one Kenneth Misner. [4]Over the next several days Bundy ***was extensively interviewed by officers from the Pensacola and Tallahassee Police Departments and the Leon County Sheriff's Office***. [5]During this time ***he revealed*** his true identity. [6]***It was learned*** that ***Bundy was wanted for escape and homicide*** in Colorado and was a suspect in thirty-six sex-related murders in the northwest United States. [7]During these interviews and thereafter, ***Bundy*** also became the prime suspect in the January 1978 murders of the Chi Omega Sorority members in Tallahassee. [8]Later ***Bundy was indicted, convicted***, and ***sentenced*** to death for the Chi Omega murders. [8]***We affirmed*** his convictions and sentences. Bundy v. State, 455 So.2d 330 (Fla. 1984), herein called Bundy v. State - I.

Table 21. A Passive Subordinate Clause Changed into an Active Subordinate Clause.

A. Original Text. From Doc. 7. Total line count: 8, Total word count: 101, Total character count: 675

[1]Since Defendants have not established that the Ineligibility Clause is open to more than one construction, it is neither necessary nor proper to examine the history of the Ineligibility Clause. *Lake County v. Rollins*, 130 U.S. 662 (1889). [2]In this instance, however, the purposes of the Framers in adopting the Ineligibility Clause support a plain language interpretation of the provision. [3]Moreover, entirely absent from the historical record is any support for Defendants' preferred "on net" interpretation of the Ineligibility Clause. [4]Nor does the historical record provide any basis whatsoever for the conclusion *that a Member's ineligibility could be "fixed" by Congress.*

B. Revised Text. Total line count: 7, Total word count: 99, Total character count: 664

[1]Since Defendants have not established that the Ineligibility Clause is open to more than one construction, it is neither necessary nor proper to examine the history of the Ineligibility Clause. *Lake County v. Rollins*, 130 U.S. 662 (1889). [2]In this instance, however, the purposes of the Framers in adopting the Ineligibility Clause support a plain language interpretation of the provision. [3]Moreover, entirely absent from the historical record is any support for Defendants' preferred "on net" interpretation of the Ineligibility Clause. [4]Nor does the historical record provide any basis whatsoever for the conclusion *that Congress could fix a Member's ineligibility.*

Strategy 19

Rephrase double or multiple negatives.

Double or multiple negatives are often wordier and harder to understand than their corresponding positive phrasing. If the sentence does not need to be phrased in the negative for precision, it should be revised into positive phrasing. Example 22A gives a sentence with a triple negative, and Example 22B gives its revision, which results in a savings of two words and is easier to understand.

Example 22
A. I request that you *not* send notices to *any* members *not* involved in the demonstrations.

Total word count: 15, Total character count: 86

B. I request that you send notices only to those members involved in the demonstrations.

Total word count: 14, Total character count: 85

Strategy 20

Shorten wordy
sentence openers.

Sometimes writers use wordy sentence (or clause) openers, such as *it is proposed that* and *there are/is*. Sentence openers can be useful to introduce new information and sometimes to emphasize information, but they can also be wordy and vague because they might not identify the agent, the person or thing performing the action. A few sentence openers that do not identify the agent, and their less wordy and more informative counterparts, are listed here:

Wordy Sentence Openers	More Concise and Informative Sentence Openers
It is noteworthy that	*We/I note that*
It is proposed that	*We/I propose that*
It was a proposal to	*The mediator proposed to*
It is recommended that	*Defendant recommends that*
It is our recommendation that	*We recommend that*
It was believed that	*We/I believed that*
It was reported that	*Officer Jones reported that*

It is our/my opinion　　　　　*We/I believe that*
It was communicated that　　*The father-in-law suggested that*

The following examples illustrate sentences that begin with wordy sentence openers. The wordy sentence opener in Example 23A does not identify the agent—that is, it does not identify who learned that Bundy was wanted for escape and homicide. Example 23A is revised in Example 23B to eliminate the wordy sentence opener and to make the sentence more informative. Also, in Example 23C, changing *thirty-six* to *36* (Strategy 9) and abbreviating *northwest* to *N.W.* (Strategy 3) combine to substantially reduce the sentence in terms of total character count.

Example 23
A. *It was learned that* Bundy was wanted for escape and homicide in Colorado and was a suspect in thirty-six sex-related murders in the northwest United States.

From Doc. 2, sentence 6 in Table 20. Total word count: 26, Total character count: 156

B. *The officers learned that* Bundy was wanted for escape and homicide in Colorado and was a suspect in thirty-six sex-related murders in the northwest United States.

Total word count: 26, Total character count: 162

C. *The officers learned that* Bundy was wanted for escape and homicide in Colorado and was a suspect in *36* sex-related murders in the *N.W.* United States.

Total word count: 26, Total character count: 149

Some wordy openers indicate the writer's opinions, such as *there is little doubt that* in Example 24A and *it is possible that* in Example 25A. When eliminating such wordy openers, other changes are often needed. In Example 24B, the adverb *undoubtedly* is a close synonym to the sentence opener, and in Example 25B, the modal *may* indicates that the writer believes the statement is not a fact. Even when the adverb and the modal are added to Examples 24B and 25B, they are still more concise than their corresponding examples with the wordy sentence openers.

Example 24

A. *There is little doubt that* Howard Lyman and the Winfrey-show employees melodramatized the "Mad Cow Disease" scare and the discussion of the question "Can it happen here?"

From Doc. 10. Total word count: 27, Total character count: 169

B. Howard Lyman and the Winfrey-show employees *undoubtedly* melodramatized the "Mad Cow Disease" scare and the discussion of the question "Can it happen here?"

Total word count: 23, Total character count: 155

Example 25

A. *It is possible that* the neighbor had seen the child picked up.

Total word count: 12, Total character count: 62

B. The neighbor *may* have seen the child picked up.

Total word count: 9, Total character count: 37

Strategy 21

Use gapping sentence structure.

Gapping is an advanced sentence structure that operates similarly to a contraction of a word. In a contraction, an apostrophe is used to replace omitted letters. In gapping, a comma is used in a sentence to replace an omitted verb.

Gapping can be applied to a sequence of clauses that: (a) are semantically similar, (b) have the same sentence structure, and (c) have identical verbs. Table 22A shows a sequence of two sentences with these features. The second and third sentences are semantically similar: each identifies the addressee to a subpoena *duces tecum*; both sentences are in passive grammar without the agent identified; and the verbs are identical (*is addressed to*). In Table 22B, the second sentence has undergone gapping: the verb has been omitted and replaced with a comma to fill the gap—a revision that has eliminated the short last line of the paragraph.

Why use gapping to shorten a paragraph? Besides reducing words and potentially reducing lines of text, gapping can enhance your credibility since this grammar reflects highly controlled, educated prose.

Table 22. Use of Gapping to Shorten the Text.

A. Original Text. From Doc. 16. Total line count: 6, Total word count: 48, Total character count: 320

[1]The Government has applied for two subpoenas *duces tecum* pursuant to Federal Rule of Criminal Procedure 17(c). [2]***The first subpoena is addressed to*** the law firm of Wachtell, Lipton, Rosen & Katz ("Wachtell, Lipton"), attorney for defendant Martha Stewart. [3]***The other subpoena is addressed to*** defendant Peter Bacanovic.

B. Revised Text. Total line count: 5, Total word count: 45, Total character count: 297

[1]The Government has applied for two subpoenas *duces tecum* pursuant to Federal Rule of Criminal Procedure 17(c). [2]***The first subpoena is addressed to*** the law firm of Wachtell, Lipton, Rosen & Katz ("Wachtell, Lipton"), attorney for defendant Martha Stewart; ***the other, to*** defendant Peter Bacanovic.

Strategy 22

Reduce emphatic phrasing and punctuation.

Emphatic phrasing and punctuation are useful to help readers notice particular pieces of information. Example 26A illustrates a sentence that uses an em dash and a resumptive modifier, a type of emphatic phrasing that repeats *effort*, which brings the readers' attention to the word. A problem with emphatic phrasing and punctuation is that the resulting sentence is wordier than a sentence without them. Therefore, to shorten the text, you can reduce emphatic phrasing and punctuation.

The revision in Example 26B decreases the emphasis and uses two fewer words than does Example 26A. The revision involves changing the resumptive modifier to a relative clause (*which includes blatant prevarication about his health status*), eliminating the repetition of *effort*, and rearranging phrases and clauses to locate the relative clause immediately after *effort*.

Example 26

A. As is set forth below, Petitioner's last-ditch *effort* to avoid the considered judgments of the courts—*an effort that includes blatant prevarication about his health status*—cannot survive scrutiny on either the law or the facts.

From Doc. 3. Total word count: 36, Total character count: 231

B. As is set forth below, to avoid the considered judgments of the courts, Petitioner's last-ditch *effort, which includes blatant prevarication about his health status,* cannot survive scrutiny on either the law or the facts.

Total word count: 34, Total character count: 221

Reduce strings of prepositional phrases.

You might catch yourself drafting sentences with strings of prepositional phrases, three or even more such phrases in a row. These strings are sometimes wordy and can be hard for readers to understand on a first reading.

For conciseness and for readability, you need to reduce strings of prepositional phrases through the use of verbs and nouns. Example 27A is the first sentence of this paragraph. It has a string of three prepositional phrases: (1) *of prepositional phrases*, (2) *through the use*, and (3) *of verbs and nouns*. In Example 27B, the string is reduced to two prepositional phrases by changing the noun *use* into a gerund, which is a noun form (*using*) of the verb *use*.

Example 27
A. For conciseness and also for readability, you need to reduce strings *of prepositional phrases through the use of verbs and phrases* that take fewer prepositions.

Total word count: 25, Total character count: 160

B. For conciseness and also for readability, you need to reduce strings *of prepositional phrases by using verbs and phrases* that take fewer prepositions.

Total word count: 23, Total character count: 150

Table 23A presents a paragraph with a short last line and a string of prepositional phrases in the last sentence. The reduction of this string shortens the paragraph by one line.

Table 23. Reduction of Multiple Prepositional Phrases.

A. Original Text. From Doc. 8, page 3. Total line count: 6, Total word count: 77, Total character count: 479

[1]In or about the first week of December, Madoff told Senior Employee No. 2 that there had been requests from clients for approximately $7 billion in redemptions, that he was struggling to obtain the liquidity necessary to meet those obligations, but that he thought that he would be able to do so. [2]According to Senior Employees, they had previously understood that the investment advisory business had assets under management ***on the order of between*** approximately $8-15 billion.

B. Revised Text. Total line count: 5, Total word count: 73, Total character count: 458

[1]In or about the first week of December, Madoff told Senior Employee No. 2 that there had been requests from clients for approximately $7 billion in redemptions, that he was struggling to obtain the liquidity necessary to meet those obligations, but that he thought that he would be able to do so. [2]According to Senior Employees, they had previously understood that the investment advisory business had assets under management ***of*** approximately $8-15 billion.

Consider omitting the optional *that*.

Independent clauses embedded inside sentences are typically marked with ***that***, which is called a ***complementizer*** or ***subordinating conjunction***. Examples 28A and 29A illustrate sentences with embedded clauses indicated by ***that***.

Example 28
A. It is undisputed ***that*** the office of U.S. Secretary of State is a "civil Office under the Authority of the United States" and the "emoluments" of that Office increased during the time Mrs. Clinton was elected to serve and did serve as U.S. Senator from the State of New York.

From Doc. 7. Total word count: 50, Total character count: 274

B. It is undisputed: the office of U.S. Secretary of State is a "civil Office under the Authority of the United States" and the "emoluments" of that Office increased during the time Mrs. Clinton was elected to serve and did serve as U.S. Senator from the State of New York.

Total word count: 49, Total character count: 270

Example 29
A. The evidence will show *that* Pete is not ready for the demands of parenthood and the sacrifices that would entail to a 20-year-old aspiring actor/model.

From Doc. 4. Total word count: 25, Total character count: 151

B. The evidence will show Pete is not ready for the demands of parenthood and the sacrifices that would entail to a 20-year-old aspiring actor/model.

Total word count: 24, Total character count: 146

That is technically optional as a complementizer. However, *that* is useful for clarity and readability, helping readers focus on the information in the embedded clause. In any case, if you are desperate for space, you can omit *that*.

Examples 28B and 29B have been revised to eliminate *that*. As shown in Example 28B, you can use a colon (:) instead of *that*—punctuation that also serves to mark the upcoming embedded clause (as does *that*), except that the colon emphasizes the information in the embedded clause. Marking an embedded clause with *that* signals syntactic subordination, which contributes to the readability of the sentence.

The omission of *that* not only can shorten the number of words and characters in the text; it might also eliminate a short last line of a paragraph, as in Table 1 (compare sentence 3 in Tables 1C and 1D in Chapter 1).

Chapter 4

Changing the Appearance of Text on the Page

Strategy 25. Change stand-alone headings into run-in headings.

Strategy 26. Omit the heading to the Introduction Section.

Strategy 27. Allow paragraph orphans and widows.

Strategy 28. Combine paragraphs.

Strategy 29. Change the size of margins, fonts, and leading.

Change stand-alone headings into run-in headings.

Headings at each level in the organizational hierarchy need to take on a consistent visual appearance. One type of heading is called *stand-alone*. A stand-alone heading is followed by text on the next line down or two lines down, such as the headings in Table 24A. Another type of heading is the *run-in* heading. A run-in heading is followed by punctuation, such as a period or a colon, and the text follows on the same line, as shown in Table 24B. Paragraph numbers can also be formatted in stand-alone or run-in style, even when the paragraphs bear only numbers.

If submission requirements do not specify otherwise, you can use run-in headings (and run-in paragraph numbers) either throughout the document or at particular levels in the organizational hierarchy. Even in the short example in Table 24B, the run-in headings save five lines.

Table 24. Examples of Stand-Alone and Run-In Headings.

A. The text uses stand-alone headings. **B.** The text uses run-in headings.

A. Original Text with Stand-Alone Headings. From Doc. 14. Total line count: 18, Total word count: 163, Total character count: 1027

I. The History of the Adam Walsh Act

[1]It is beyond question that sexual victimization, particularly of children, is a major problem in this country. [2]As a result of the significant media attention that this problem has received in recent decades, the horrific crimes suffered by children such as Jacob Wetterling, Adam Walsh, Megan Kanka, and Polly Klaas, weigh heavily on America's collective . . .

II. Factual Background

[3]Defendant Robert Powers is a 43-year-old man with an IQ of 68 and a second-grade reading level. In 1995, he was convicted under South Carolina law of "Assault to Commit Sex Crimes". [4]In compliance with South Carolina law, Mr. Powers registered as a sex offender on November 13, 1995. [5]Mr. Powers moved to Florida in 2007 to live with his mother in Orlando. He failed to register as a sex offender in Florida, as required by Florida Statute . . .

III. Legal Analysis

[6]Defendant is charged with violating 18 U.S.C. § 2250(a) ("§ 2250(a)"), which provides . . .

B. Revised Text with Run-In Headings. Total line count: 13, Total word count: 163, Total character count: 986

I. The History of the Adam Walsh Act. [1]It is beyond question that sexual victimization, particularly of children, is a major problem in this country. [2]As a result of the significant media attention that this problem has received in recent decades, the horrific crimes suffered by children such as Jacob Wetterling, Adam Walsh, Megan Kanka, and Polly Klaas, weigh heavily on America's collective . . .

II. Factual Background. [3]Defendant Robert Powers is a 43-year-old man with an IQ of 68 and a second-grade reading level. In 1995, he was convicted under South Carolina law of "Assault to Commit Sex Crimes". [4]In compliance with South Carolina law, Mr. Powers registered as a sex offender on November 13, 1995. [5]Mr. Powers moved to Florida in 2007 to live with his mother in Orlando. He failed to register as a sex offender in Florida, as required by Florida Statute **. . .**

III. Legal Analysis. [6]Defendant is charged with violating 18 U.S.C. § 2250(a) ("§ 2250(a)"), which provides . . .

Strategy 26

Omit the heading to the Introduction Section.

Many legal documents not submitted to courts, such as employee manuals and settlement brochures, might have introductions with headings. Likewise, sections and subsections within legal documents might have introductions with headings. To shorten the text, the heading *Introduction,* along with any section number, can be omitted. Readers recognize that any paragraph(s) between the title and the first substantive heading comprises an introduction. Note: If you remove the heading *Introduction* and its section number, you need to revise all subsequent section numbers.

Allow paragraph orphans and widows.

Some court rules specify that pleadings filed with the court cannot have just one line of a paragraph at the very bottom or the very top of a page. The term ***paragraph orphan*** is the first line of a paragraph that is at the bottom of a page, with the rest of its paragraph continuing on the next page, and the term ***paragraph widow*** is the last line of a paragraph at the top of a page, with the rest of its paragraph on the bottom of the previous page.

Word-processing programs are often set to avoid paragraph orphans and widows by controlling where paragraphs break across pages. However, the programs create wasted space when they insert lines at the bottom of a page to eliminate orphans and widows. To remove these blank lines and, thus, to shorten your legal document, you can adjust your word-processing program[1] so that it allows widows and orphans.

---

1. In Microsoft Word 2003, for example, to deactivate the widow/orphan feature globally, you first select all of the text in the document (control + A) and then follow Format > Paragraph > Line and Page Breaks. A pop-up menu appears. To

Even if submission requirements do not allow widows and orphans, you can still adjust your word-processing program to allow them. You can apply text-shortening strategies in this handbook, which will eliminate the last lines of paragraphs and shift paragraphs higher on a page, resulting in the natural elimination of orphans and widows while not adding any extra space. For example, Table 25 shows two consecutive pages (pages 5 and 6), the second of which has a widow. Revising page 5 to change *approximately* to *about* (Strategy 1 applied to line 23) eliminates both the short last line of the paragraph and the paragraph widow. The resulting shorter text is shown in Table 26. However, if submission requirements do not allow paragraphs to start at the top of a page, additional editing of text on page 5 is needed.

deactivate orphans and widows in order to save space, you uncheck the widow/orphan feature. To deactivate the orphan-widow feature for a particular paragraph only, place the cursor in the paragraph, and then follow Format > Paragraph > Line and Page Breaks.

Table 25. The Top of a Page with a Paragraph Widow.

Modified from Doc. 4. The last line was left blank, which forced the last line of the paragraph to the top of the next page. Names, dates, exhibit numbers, and hours have been changed for confidentiality.

. . .

17 issues, based on statements he has made about seeking his child. [Exhibit 6,

18 Pete Peters Dated November 4, 2008]. The bottom line is this: Since the date of

19 birth on February 1, 2007, to the date of filing this Petition on February 6,

20 2009, there have been approximately 735 days. Multiplied by 24—the number

21 of hours in a day—there have been 17,640 hours. During that time Pete has not

22 had any time alone with the baby, and the approximate total number of hours

23 Pete has had the baby with the assistance of his family comes to ***approximately***

24 //

25 Petition for Custody

26 Doe v. Doe, Case No. XXXX

    Page 5

---

1 ***152 hours.***

2   All of these facts warrant a finding that 100% of legal and physical custody

3 should be awarded to Cindy with scheduled visitation for Pete.

4

. . .

25 Petition for Custody

26 Doe v. Doe, Case No. XXXX

    Page 6

Table 26. Elimination of the Paragraph Widow from Table 25.

Modified from Doc. 4. The paragraph widow in Table 25, page 6, line 1 was eliminated by the application of Strategy 1 to line 23, where *approximately* was changed to *about*.

. . .

17 issues, based on statements he has made about seeking his child. [Exhibit 6,
18 Pete Peters Dated November 4, 2008]. The bottom line is this: Since the date of
19 birth on February 1, 2007, to the date of filing this Petition on February 6,
20 2009, there have been approximately 735 days. Multiplied by 24—the number
21 of hours in a day—there have been 17,640 hours. During that time Pete has not
22 had any time alone with the baby, and the approximate total number of hours
23 Pete has had the baby with the assistance of his family comes to *about*
24 152 hours.
25 Petition for Custody
26 Doe v. Doe, Case No. XXXX
Page 5

1   All of these facts warrant a finding that 100% of legal and physical custody
2 should be awarded to Cindy with scheduled visitation for Pete.
3
4

. . .

25 Petition for Custody
26 Doe v. Doe, Case No. XXXX
Page 6

Strategy 28

Combine paragraphs.

One way to save space is to combine two consecutive paragraphs into one. However, not just any two consecutive paragraphs should be combined. They each need to be relatively short, and they need to be about the same or closely related topics.

When combining such paragraphs to save space, you may need to revise the resulting paragraph in order for it to retain features of *a powerful paragraph*. A powerful paragraph is organized in a particular way: its opening sentence(s) gives the topic of the combined paragraph or the most important information in the combined paragraph. In many cases, the most important information can be repeated (and rephrased) at the end of the paragraph since information at the end of a paragraph is more salient than information in its middle.

Unfortunately, even though combining paragraphs can save space, the savings comes with a price: the longer combined paragraph might have organizational problems or other problems that will decrease its readability. Four additional editing strategies can compensate for organizational or readability problems in the combined paragraph:

    (1) revise the first couple of sentences in the combined paragraph so that they capture the most important information of the original two paragraphs,

    (2) omit the topic sentence of the second paragraph (assuming the second paragraph has a topic sentence),

    (3) omit any redundant information across the original two paragraphs, and

    (4) add organizational cues to help readers follow the organization of the combined paragraph.

Table 27A presents two related paragraphs that can be combined to reduce the total line and word counts. Table 27B gives the combined paragraph. Its first sentence now includes information that comprises the lead-in to a list (*only two witnesses have come forth*), thus changing the first sentence into a topic sentence. In addition, itemization marks each item in the list, making the organization of the combined paragraph more apparent. The combined paragraph in Table 27B results in a savings of one line.

Table 27. Two Paragraphs Combined to Shorten the Text.

A. The original organization, with the information presented in two paragraphs.
B. The combined paragraph with compensatory bold font, redundant information eliminated, and numbers used as organizational cues.

A. Original Text. From Doc. 2. Total line count: 19 lines, Total word count: 196, Total character count: 1132

[1]Prior to Bundy's indictment on July 21, 1978, for the Leach murder and kidnapping, only one witness placed Bundy and the white van at the scene of the Lake City Junior High School on the morning of February 9, 1978. [2]Chuck Edenfield, a school crossing guard at the junior high school, testified that he saw a man whom he identified as Bundy driving a white van in front of the school.

[3]The state's one eyewitness to the abduction of Kimberly Leach was Clarence Anderson. [4]On July 18, 1978, Anderson reported to the Lake City Police Department that the profile of a person he had seen on a television newscast bore a striking resemblance to the man that he had observed with a girl near the Lake City Junior High School several months earlier. [5]Assistant State Attorney Dekle asked Anderson to undergo hypnosis to refresh his memory. [6]Anderson agreed and was hypnotized twice. [7]Thereafter, he stated that on February 9, 1978, he noticed a man leading a young girl into a white van near the Lake City Junior High School. [8]Anderson identified the young girl as Kimberly Leach and the man in the van as Theodore Bundy.

B. Revised Text. Total line count: 18 lines, Total word count: 200, Total character count: 1143

[1]Prior to Bundy's indictment on July 21, 1978, for the Leach murder and kidnapping, only two witnesses came forth. *(1)* [2]Chuck Edenfield, a school-crossing guard at the junior high school, placed Bundy and the white van at the scene of the Lake City Junior High School on the morning of February 9, 1978. [3]He testified that he saw a man whom he identified as Bundy driving a white van in front of the school. *(2)* [4]The state's one eyewitness to the abduction of Kimberly Leach was Clarence Anderson. [5]On July 18, 1978, Anderson reported to the Lake City Police Department that the profile of a person he had seen on a television newscast bore a striking resemblance to the man that he had observed with a girl near the Lake City Junior High School several months earlier. [6]Assistant State Attorney Dekle asked Anderson to undergo hypnosis to refresh his memory. [7]Anderson agreed and was hypnotized twice. [8]Thereafter, he stated that on February 9, 1978, he noticed a man leading a young girl into a white van near the Lake City Junior High School. [9]He identified the young girl as Kimberly Leach and the man in the van as Theodore Bundy.

Strategy 29

Change the size of margins, fonts, and leading.

Three ways to save space are to modify the size of fonts, margins, and leading[1] (the vertical spacing between lines) within and across (sub)sections and paragraphs. However, even though these changes can save space, they may violate requirements for legal documents submitted to federal and state courts or to journals, in which case you need to apply other strategies.

Changing the size of margins, fonts, and leading sometimes creates other problems. A smaller font or reduced leading might not be as legible as a larger font. In addition, text in a font without serifs (sans serifs), such as **Arial**, may be harder to read than text in a font with serifs, such as **Times New Roman**. Interestingly, online, just the reverse is true: sans-serif fonts are easier to read

---

1. In Microsoft Word 2003, leading can be accessed through the drop-down Format menu (Format > Paragraph > Indents and Spacing > Spacing field).

than fonts with serifs. If you are working on a document that will only be read online, you need to consider a sans-serif font.

In the absence of requirements for a particular legal document, the following font styles and sizes can create a legible text: (1) for section headings Arial or Helvetica 11-point font; (2) for text, Times New Roman 12-point font; (3) for text in legends to visuals, Times New Roman 11-point font or Arial 10-point font; (4) for leading, 0 points in the paragraph spacing field; and (5) for margins, 1.0" all around; however, if the legal document will be bound, use a left-hand margin of 1.5".

In one format style for a vertical list, each item is indented a few characters, presumably to indicate the subordination of the list to the paragraph in which it occurs. Table 28A gives a paragraph and a subordinate list with extreme indentation. By changing the indentation to that as shown in Table 28B, a savings of three lines is realized.

To give all paragraphs with vertical lists the same look in a document, you need to use the same indentation style.

Table 28. Margins of Vertical List Changed to Shorten the Text.

A. The original layout, with a bulleted vertical list with indented margins. **B.** The revised layout with only the first line of each item indented.

A. Original Text. From Doc. 18. Total line count: 20, Total word count: 213, Total character count: 1356

2. [1]As a company that now directly competes with craigslist through its Kijiji classified ads website launched in the United States in 2007, eBay cannot deny that it has certain duties under the law. [2]Yet eBay has chosen to ignore these duties and, without this Court's intervention, it will continue to do so. [3]By way of example, eBay has engaged in the following wrongful behavior:

- [4]In the months leading up to the U.S. launch of its competing Kijiji site (referred to inside eBay as the "craigslist killer'), eBay used its shareholder status to plant on craigslist's board of directors the individual responsible for launching and/or operating Kijiji and other eBay classifieds properties in Europe;

- [5]Later recognizing the antitrust risk of having a Kijiji insider serve on craigslist's board, eBay withdrew him, but then proceeded to nominate a second Kijiji insider, namely the individual responsible for Kijiji's worldwide competition policy;

- [6]Throughout its tenure as a craigslist shareholder, under the guise of shareholder requests for information, eBay has hounded craigslist with improper demands for confidential craigslist information which could be used for anticompetitive purposes; and

- [7]eBay has used craigslist's mark and name in commerce to confuse the public and illegally divert internet traffic from craigslist to eBay and its Kijiji site.

B. Revised Text. Total line count: 17 lines, Total word count: 213, Total character count: 1365

2. [1]As a company that now directly competes with craigslist through its Kijiji classified ads website launched in the United States in 2007, eBay cannot deny that it has certain duties under the law. [2]Yet eBay has chosen to ignore these duties and, without this Court's Intervention, it will continue to do so. [3]By way of example, eBay has engaged in the following wrongful behavior:

- [4]In the months leading up to the U.S. launch of its competing Kijiji site (referred to inside eBay as the "craigslist killer"), eBay used its shareholder status to plant on craigslist's board of directors the individual responsible for launching and/or operating Kijiji and other eBay classifieds properties in Europe;
- [5]Later recognizing the antitrust risk of having a Kijiji insider serve on craigslist's board, eBay withdrew him, but then proceeded to nominate a second Kijiji insider, namely the individual responsible for Kijiji's worldwide competition policy;
- [6]Throughout its tenure as a craigslist shareholder, under the guise of shareholder requests for information, eBay has hounded craigslist with improper demands for confidential craigslist information which could be used for anticompetitive purposes; and
- [7]eBay has used craigslist's mark and name in commerce to confuse the public and illegally divert internet traffic from craigslist to eBay and its Kijiji site.

Chapter 5

Cutting Content

Strategy 30. Omit redundant or unnecessary information.

Strategy 31. Eliminate forecast statements in introductions.

Strategy 32. Shorten the introduction to quotes 50 words and longer, and shorten the quotes.

Strategy 33. Reduce examples.

Strategy 34. Consider using visuals to shorten the text.

Strategy 35. Omit irrelevant and non-useful information.

Strategy 30

Omit redundant or unnecessary information.

A common problem with legal documents is that they have redundant or unnecessary information. To shorten the text, you need to omit such superfluous information.

Many examples in this handbook are wordy, in part due to redundant or unnecessary information. Example 30A (from Table 4) has a few such problems: (1) **on the books** is unnecessary information since it adds no new information to the sentence, (2) numbers written in both words and numerals are redundant, and (3) **at the time of his birth** is redundant with **was born** earlier in the sentence. Example 30B gives a revision that eliminates the redundant and unnecessary information, which results in a savings of nine words and 39 characters.

Example 30

A. [1]If in fact Obama was born in Kenya, the laws **on the books at the time of his birth** stated if a child is born abroad and one parent was a U.S. Citizen, which would have been his mother, Stanley Ann Dunham, she would have had to live *ten (10)* years in the U.S., *five (5)* of which were after the age of *fourteen (14)*.

From Doc. 1, sentence 1 in Table 4. Total word count: 65, Total character count: 315

B. [1]If in fact Obama was born in Kenya, the laws *at that time* stated if a child is born abroad and one parent was a U.S. Citizen, which would have been his mother, Stanley Ann Dunham, she would have had to live *ten* years in the U.S., *five* of which were after the age of *fourteen*.

Total word count: 56, Total character count: 276

Example 31A also has redundant information that can be eliminated to shorten the text. The term *negotiated a contract* has unnecessary words since the notion of negotiation is not necessary in this passage, so the term is shortened to its verb equivalent *contracted* (Strategy 5) in Example 31B. In addition, the term *bonus amounts* is redundant; a bonus is an amount, so just the term *bonuses* can be used, as shown in Example 31B. These two changes reduce the total word count by three.

Example 31
A. [1]In 2004, Vick *negotiated a contract* with the Atlanta Falcons to play football for the team through 2014. [2]In addition to a yearly salary, the contract included two roster bonuses—one for 2005 ($22.5 million) and one for 2006 ($7 million). [3]The contract stated that the *bonus amounts* would be additional consideration for the execution of the long-term player contract, provided that (1) Vick . . .

From Doc. 17, sentences 1–3 in Table 7. Total word count: 64, Total character count: 396

B. [1]In 2004, Vick *contracted* with the Atlanta Falcons to play football for the team through 2014. [2]In addition to a yearly salary, the contract included two roster bonuses—one for 2005 ($22.5 million) and one for 2006 ($7 million). [3]The contract stated that the *bonuses* would be additional consideration for the execution of the long-term player contract, provided that (1) Vick . . .

Total word count: 61, Total character count: 377

In Example 32A, the phrase *the scene of* is redundant with *the Lake City Junior High*. In Example 32B, this redundancy has been eliminated, for a savings of three words. Also, by substituting *Prior to* with *Before* (Strategy 1), another word can be saved.

Example 32

A. [1]*Prior to* Bundy's indictment on July 21, 1978, for the Leach murder and kidnapping, only one witness placed Bundy and the white van at *the scene of the Lake City Junior High School* on the morning of February 9, 1978.

From Doc. 2, sentence 1 in Table 27. Total word count: 40, Total character count: 216

B. [1]*Before* Bundy's indictment on July 21, 1978, for the Leach murder and kidnapping, only one witness placed Bundy and the white van *at the Lake City Junior High School* on the morning of February 9, 1978.

Total word count: 36, Total character count: 201

Example 33A has redundant information about *the court*, which can be eliminated. In Example 33B, the text is shortened by six words through the creation of a lead-in (with the information about the court) and a list.

Example 33

A. [1]The district court rested its decision on *several bases*. [2]*First, the district court questioned the applicability* of the statute to live "fed cattle." [3]*Second, the court disputed* whether the plaintiffs' cattle "perished" or "decayed beyond marketability" as required for statutory protection.

From Doc. 10. Total word count: 41, Total character count: 295

B. [3]The district court rested its decision on *two bases*: *(1)* the applicability of the statute to live "fed cattle" *and* *(2)* whether the plaintiffs' cattle "perished" or "decayed beyond marketability" as required for statutory protection.

Total word count: 35, Total character count: 235

If information needs to be repeated in a legal document, a cross-reference can be used to take the reader to the first mention of the information, which signals a deliberate repetition of content. You need to use a cross-reference where the same facts are alleged for each claim. Example 34 is a sentence from a pleading, which refers back to a fact section in a previous claim of a complaint.

Example 34

Paragraphs 1 through 24 are realleged and incorporated by reference as if set forth fully in this paragraph.

Strategy 31

Eliminate forecast statements in introductions.

The introduction to a legal document might use a forecast statement to help orient readers to the upcoming content. A forecast statement identifies the organization of topics in the document and the type and purpose of the document.

When you are reducing content, the forecast statement is one of the most expendable types of information in a legal document since it does not advance the content under discussion. Example 35A gives an introduction from an attorney's correspondence, with the forecast statement in bold italics. This forecast statement is eliminated in Example 35B, saving 30 words and two lines.

Example 35
A. [1]I am attaching the proposal that your partner's attorney emailed to me this morning. [2]It consists of 6 pages plus 2 supplements, which appear to be bank records. [3]*In my letter to you, I first highlight key points in the proposal and*

I evaluate each point. [4]*You will find my recommended response in the last paragraph of this letter.* [5]Could you read the entire proposal and then call me at your earliest convenience?

Total word count: 73, Total character count: 420

B. [1]I am attaching the proposal that your partner's attorney just emailed to me. [2]It consists of 6 pages plus 2 supplements, which appear to be bank records. [3]Could you read the entire proposal and then call me at your earliest convenience?

Total word count: 41, Total character count: 239

Strategy 32

Shorten the introduction to quotes 50 words and longer, and shorten the quotes.

Legal documents submitted to a federal or state court are typically double-spaced throughout, except for quoted material 50 words or longer, which is presented in single-spaced block style and is fully indented.[1] The source of the quoted material is then identified after another blank line. Further, if the blocked quote omits a paragraph, the protocol is to skip a line, add ellipses on a separate line to indicate the skipped paragraph, and then skip another line. A blocked quote, whether or not it includes blank lines for omitted paragraphs, can significantly lengthen the text.

---

1. *The Bluebook: A Uniform System of Citation* R. B12, at page 23 and R. 5.2, at pages 68–69 (Columbia Law Review Ass'n et al. eds., 18th ed. 2005).

To avoid wasted space resulting from a blocked quotation that is 50 words or longer, the introduction (lead-in) to the direct quote and the direct quote need to be evaluated for unnecessary or redundant content. If the lead-in essentially repeats or rephrases the direct quote, the lead-in or the quote can be reduced. Another alternative is to eliminate the redundant information in the quote, which might reduce it to fewer than 50 words. In that case, the blocked layout is no longer required, and the information can be integrated into the paragraph.

In Table 29A, the paragraph includes a lead-in to the quote with much of the same information that begins the quote. The lead-in is useful in introducing the quote, but the extent of repetition between the lead-in and the quoted text is excessive. By omitting the redundant information from the quote (this strategy) and by using shorter synonyms for long terms (Strategy 1), the quote is reduced to 49 words. At this shorter length, it can be integrated into the existing paragraph, as shown in Table 29B. These edits reduce the text by nine lines and 16 words.

In Table 30A, information that identifies the courts in the blocked quote is not needed and extends the quote to over 49 words. The paragraph focuses on criteria for the court to determine whether the defendant will likely violate securities laws again; the information about the court is useful, but the court is not itself a criterion. The revision in Table 30B omits information on the court, which reduces the quote to 46 words, a length that allows the integration of the quote into the paragraph. This revision significantly reduces the total number of lines, words, and characters.

Table 29. Shortening a Blocked Quotation.

A. Original Text. From Doc. 2. Total line count: 30, Total word count: 227, Total character count: 1616

[1]As his first point on appeal Bundy argues that the trial judge erred in denying Bundy's several motions to suppress the testimony of certain witnesses whose recall had been affected or altered by hypnosis. [2]The defense contended that due to the lapse of time between the disappearance of the Leach girl and the revelation of Anderson almost six months later, the massive amount of information about the events that Anderson had ingested during that period of time, and the blatant misuse of hypnosis by those who had facilitated the sessions, a substantial likelihood of an irreparable in-court misidentification of Bundy by Anderson would occur. [3]In his argument before the trial court, Bundy relied on the case of *Neil v. Biggers*, 409 U.S. 188 (1972). [4]In *Neil v. Biggers* the United States Supreme Court outlined the **factors to be considered by the trial court in determining whether an identification was reliable even though the confrontation procedure was suggestive.** [5]**The Court stated:**

> **[T]he factors to be considered in evaluating the likelihood of misidentification include the** opportunity of the witness to view the criminal at the time of the crime, the witness' degree of attention, the accuracy of the witness' prior description of the criminal, **the level** of certainty demonstrated by the witness at the confrontation, and **the length of** time between the crime and the confrontation.

Id. at 199-200.

B. Revised Text. Total line count: 21, Total word count: 209, Total character count: 1294

[1]As his first point on appeal Bundy argues that the trial judge erred in denying Bundy's several motions to suppress the testimony of certain witnesses whose recall had been affected or altered by hypnosis. [2]The defense contended that due to the lapse of time between the disappearance of the Leach girl and the revelation of Anderson almost six months later, the massive amount of information about the events that Anderson had ingested during that period of time, and the blatant misuse of hypnosis by those who had facilitated the sessions, a substantial likelihood of an irreparable in-court misidentification of Bundy by Anderson would occur. [3]In his argument before the trial court, Bundy relied on the case of *Neil v. Biggers*, 409 U.S. 188 (1972). [4]***In Neil v. Biggers the United States Supreme Court outlined the factors to be considered by the trial court in determining whether an identification was reliable even though the confrontation procedure was suggestive:*** ". . . opportunity of the witness to view the criminal at the time of the crime, the witness' degree of attention, the accuracy of the witness' prior description of the criminal, *[degree]* of certainty demonstrated by the witness at the confrontation, and . . . time between the crime and the confrontation." *Id.* at 199-200.

Table 30. Eliminating Nonessential Information from Quotes.
Ellipses in the blocked quote are in the original.

A. Original Text. From Doc. 8. Total line count: 15, Total word count: 163, Total character count: 1113

[1]In determining whether to grant emergency relief, courts consider the likelihood that, unless enjoined, a defendant will violate the securities laws again. *SEC v. Cavanagh*, 155 F.3d at 135. [2]As the Second Circuit instructed in Management Dynamics, Inc.:

> Certainly, the commission of past illegal conduct is highly suggestive of the likelihood of future violations. . . [F]actors suggesting that the infraction might not have been an isolated occurrence are always relevant. . . ***Moreover, appellate courts have repeatedly cautioned that*** cessation of illegal activity does not ipso facto justify the denial of an injunction.

515 F.2d at 807. [3]In assessing likelihood of repetition, courts also look to such factors as the character of the violation, the degree of scienter involved, and the degree to which a defendant's occupation of activities may present future opportunities to violate the law. E.g., *Cavanagh*, 155 F.3d at 135; *SEC v. Commonwealth Chem. Sees., Inc.*, 574 F.2d 90, 100-01 (2d Cir. 1978); *SEC v. Musella*, 578 F. Supp. 425, 444 (S.D.N.Y. 1984).

B. Revised Text: Total line count: 11, Total word count: 157, Total character count: 1012

[1]In determining whether to grant emergency relief, courts consider the likelihood that, unless enjoined, a defendant will violate the securities laws again. *SEC v. Cavanagh*, 155 F.3d at 135. [2]As the Second Circuit instructed in Management Dynamics, Inc.: "Certainly, the commission of past illegal conduct is highly suggestive of the likelihood of future violations. . . [F]actors suggesting that the infraction might not have been an isolated occurrence are always relevant. . . *[and]* cessation of illegal activity does not ipso facto justify the denial of an injunction." 515 F.2d at 807. [3]In assessing likelihood of repetition, courts also look to such factors as the character of the violation, the degree of scienter involved, and the degree to which a defendant's occupation of activities may present future opportunities to violate the law. E.g., *Cavanagh*, 155 F.3d at 135; *SEC v. Commonwealth Chem. Sees., Inc.*, 574 F.2d 90, 100-01 (2d Cir. 1978); *SEC v. Musella*, 578 F. Supp. 425, 444 (S.D.N.Y. 1984).

Reduce examples.

You may want to include long lists of examples to drive home a point. However, such lists lengthen the text. One way to shorten the text is to reduce the number of examples. To reinforce a point that you are making, you need to select those examples that are the most important and the most representative. In Table 31A, the last two items (*urchin and abalone*) can be omitted, which eliminates the last line and two words in the paragraph, as shown in Table 31B.

Table 31. A Paragraph Shortened by Reducing the Number of Examples.

A. Original Text. From Doc. 5. Total line count: 9, Total word count: 62, Total character count: 435

[1]The PCFFA's members include small- and medium-sized family businesses whose operations range from commercial fishing vessels in distant grounds to small, trailerable boats that work nearshore waters. [2]They harvest a wide variety of ocean seafood, including fresh wild salmon, Dungeness and rock crab, squid, herring, sword fish, shark, blackcod, rockfish, albacore, sea cucumber, California halibut and flounder, *urchin and abalone*.

B. Revised Text. Total line count: 8, Total word count: 60, Total character count: 420

[1]The PCFFA's members include small- and medium-sized family businesses whose operations range from commercial fishing vessels in distant grounds to small, trailerable boats that work nearshore waters. [2]They harvest a wide variety of ocean seafood, including fresh wild salmon, Dungeness and rock crab, squid, herring, sword fish, shark, blackcod, rockfish, albacore, sea cucumber, *and* California halibut and flounder.

Consider using visuals to shorten the text.

Presenting information in a visual, such as a figure or a table, could shorten the text. For example, Table 32A presents a section from an employee handbook, and Table 32B presents a revision that uses a table. The revision has fewer lines, words, and characters than the original.

Even though document length can be reduced with a visual, you need to evaluate whether its inclusion is appropriate, given the audience and submission requirements. Many legal authorities do not give requirements for visuals that will be included in a legal document, in which case you can turn to scientific- and technical-writing authorities[1] for guidance.

Very briefly, a visual needs a heading, which consists of a number and a title. However, if there is only one visual in the document, the number is not needed. Any labels on the visual

---

1. *See, e.g.*, SCIENTIFIC STYLE AND FORMAT: THE CSE MANUAL FOR AUTHORS, EDITORS, AND PUBLISHERS (Council of Science Editors, eds., 7th ed., Rockefeller University Press 2006); MIKE MARKEL, TECHNICAL COMMUNICATION (9th ed., Bedford/St. Martin's Press 2010).

need to repeat key terms from in the text. For example, the text in Table 32 uses the terms *early closure*, *delayed opening*, and *full closure*, and these terms are also used for the column headings.

A visual might also need a legend, which is a paragraph that gives information to help readers understand the visual—like the legend of a map, which shows scale. Titles, labels, captions, and legends to visuals need to be brief since their phrasing can also affect the length of documents.

The design, layout, and use of visuals in a text are often complex. The following strategies are offered as minimal introduction to the use of visuals to save space and to achieve a readable text.

(a) Introduce the visual in the text before readers encounter it. In this way, you can introduce the visual and explain features that will help readers better understand it. If there is only one visual, you can refer to it by *the visual*, *the figure*, or *the table* as appropriate, not by its title, which will take more space. If there are multiple visuals, you can concisely refer to one by its type and number, such as *Table 2*.

(b) Discuss only critical features of the visual. If the visual is self-explanatory and uncomplicated, you can introduce it without explaining it, such as in Table 32. If you need to explain the visual, you select for discussion those critical features that will help your readers understand it. The features you discuss should be labeled on the visual.

(c) Restructure or redesign the visual. A visual needs to be simple in design and uncluttered, and it may need to be restructured to take less space. This strategy involves examining its content and determining whether the visual is ***space-worthy***—that is, whether the content of the visual warrants the space it occupies. Sometimes the visual is unnecessarily detailed and consumes too much space for the type of information it conveys, in which case you need to simplify it, such as by removing a background grid from a chart.

Another problem is that the content of a visual may be space-worthy and appropriately detailed, but the white space that frames it may be so wide that the entire visual consumes unnecessary space. In this situation, you need to reduce the surrounding white space.

(d) Wrap text around visuals. If a visual extends to less than three-fourths across the page, you can wrap text around it and its legend. You may need to change the default in your word-processing program in order to achieve the wrap-around style.[2] You can introduce a visual with wrapped text, either before the visual or within the wrapped text. Another strategy to save space is to locate the heading (and legend) to the side of the visual, rather than under it.

---

2. In Microsoft Word 2003, for example, once the visual is placed in the text, you change the default through the Table drop-down menu (Table > Table Properties > Table > Text Wrapping).

Table 32. Use of a Table to Shorten the Total Number of Lines and Total Word Count.

Line length varies from original to fit dimension of Table 32.

A. Original Text. From Doc. 5. Total lines of text: 32, Total word count: 319, Total character count: 1884

Emergency Closing/Inclement Weather

At times, emergencies such as severe weather, fires, power failures, or earthquakes can disrupt clinic operations. In extreme cases, these circumstances may require the closing of a work facility. Each division has a notification system set up for their staff and physicians that is coordinated by the Director and communicated to the staff and physicians. The TOC website will also be updated to reflect any closed clinics. Please note that this policy applies only when TOC actually closes a facility, not when your supervisor merely asks you whether you want to go home voluntarily.

Early Closure: if an early closure is declared, non-exempt and exempt, regular employees currently working will be paid to the end of their shift. Those non-exempt employees required to remain will be paid at a rate of time and one-half for hours worked after the early closure.

Delayed Opening: If a delayed opening is declared, non-exempt, regular employees will be paid only for hours actually worked. If an exempt employee works less than half of their day, they are required to use a half day of PTO if available.

Full Closure: If a full closure is declared, non-exempt, regular employees will be unpaid unless the supervisors allow the time to be made up. Exempt employees are required to use PTO and if they do not have PTO, they will be paid in accordance with wage and hour law.

Regular, non-exempt employees who do not report to work or arrive late during a declared inclement weather/emergency closure have the option of using PTO or unpaid time to make up the missed hours.

Exempt employees who work any portion of the workweek will be paid for the full week (salary and/or PTO) except for full days that the employee does not come in to work for personal reasons. if no work is performed in the week, the employee will not be paid their salary.

B. Revised Text. From Doc. 6. Total lines of text: 30, Total word count: 262; Total character count: 1562

Emergency Closing/Inclement Weather

At times, emergencies such as severe weather, fires, power failures, or earthquakes can disrupt clinic operations. In extreme cases, these circumstances may require the closing of a work facility. Each division has a notification system set up for their staff and physicians that is coordinated by the Director and communicated to the staff and physicians. The TOC website will also be updated to reflect any closed clinics. Please note that this policy applies only when TOC actually closes a facility, not when your supervisor merely asks you whether you want to go home voluntarily.

	Early Closure	**Delayed Opening**	**Full Closure**
Non-exempt Regular Employees	Paid to the end of the shift; if required to remain, paid at time and one-half worked after early closure.	Paid only for hours actually worked.	Unpaid unless the supervisors allow the time to be made up
Exempt Employees	Same as non-exempt regular employee.	If worked less than half of their day, must use a half day of PTO if available	Must use PTO; if PTO unavailable, paid according to wage-and-hour law.

Regular, non-exempt employees who do not report to work or arrive late during a declared inclement weather/emergency closure have the option of using PTO or unpaid time to make up the missed hours.

Exempt employees who work any portion of the workweek will be paid for the full week (salary and/or PTO) except for full days that the employee does not come in to work for personal reasons. if no work is performed in the week, the employee will not be paid their salary.

Omit irrelevant and non-useful information.

After applying every strategy in this handbook and any others that you can think of, you might still have a legal document that is too long for submission requirements. If so, then a last resort is to omit the least relevant and the least useful information (see also Strategy 31 on omission of forecast statements, which are a type of nonsubstantive content).

The content of a legal document obviously varies, depending on its type, purpose, and audience. To shorten a legal document, the information that you select for omission should not harm: (a) any of your legal arguments, not only in the document but those you intend to use in future related documents, (b) the readability of the text, or (c) the clarity of the text. To shorten a legal document, it is expedient to identify the most important information and then to evaluate the remaining information for possible elimination. Here is a list of information that probably cannot be omitted without harming legal argumentation, readability, or clarity.

1. Relevant law. If a particular law is relevant to the purpose of the legal document or to the case (either to your case or your opposing party's case), you should retain the law. Relevant law covers statutes, administrative rules, case law, and other points of authorities, and it includes: (a) law that supports your position, (b) law that does not support your opposing party's position, and (c) law that you know is contrary to your position.

Certain legal documents have particular sections where you cite the relevant law, such as in **Points of Authority** in a complaint. Other legal documents have particular sections where you discuss how the law applies to the facts of the case, which is sometimes called the **Legal Argument**. When you retain the law, you need to consider how much to present and in what style. Styles include: quoting relevant statutory law, quoting other relevant law, paraphrasing nonstatutory law, listing the relevant law (e.g., in a **Points of Authority** section), or footnoting the law. The following suggestion requires your evaluation of the law, relative to the facts of your case:

> *The more central or the more controversial the particular relevant law is to the disposition of your case, the more you need to quote it.*

Sometimes you will need to retain the *prima facie* elements (and facts that relate to the *prima facie* elements). You also need to retain information that pinpoints which part of the authority is directly relevant—not just a case name, for example, but the relevant holding from the case. If you anticipate your opposing party using a law that you consider not relevant, then you also need to address it since your opposing party has made it relevant to the case. Also, dicta that may support the relevancy of the law to your case, such as relevant legislative history, need to be retained.

2. Statement of facts. Whenever you present facts of a case—whether it be in a **Fact** section of a complaint or in a short paragraph in a letter—you need to present your facts as a *story* that reflects at least three features: (a) relevant time and space information; (b) facts relevant to the case; and (c) facts that help the story cohere, that are needed for clarity, or are needed for readability.

(a) Relevant time and space information. The presentation of facts requires that you tell a coherent story. Storytelling involves chronological order. Thus, whenever giving facts of your case, your plan should be to use them to tell a believable, coherent story.

Whether telling the entire story or excerpts, there are certain words and phrases that clarify the sequence of the events; these *chronological markers* should not be omitted. A few chronological markers are *before, after, later, then, next, prior to, subsequent to, in, while,* and *during.* Table 33 at the end of this strategy gives an excerpt from a statement of facts termed **STATEMENT** in an *amicus curiae.* In the first paragraph alone, there are seven chronological markers: *for many years, in 1985, after Exxon. . . , lasted 28 days, after which, shortly,* and *after his reinstatement.* These terms help tell a coherent story, are not redundant (Strategy 30), and should not be eliminated. However, the seven chronological markers in the first paragraph are in clear contrast to two chronological markers in paragraph 2 (*eventually* and *on the night*) and two in paragraph 3 (*eventually* and *to date*). Just the sheer number of chronological markers reveals the lack of specific information in paragraphs 2 and 3.

Coherence also involves including enough spatial information at each time point so that it is easy for the reader to follow the timeline of events. In Table 33, spatial markers include: *on Exxon supertankers*, *to an alcohol treatment program*, *the EXXON VALDEZ*, *through the difficult parts of Prince William Sound*, and *into Bligh Reef*. If an event in the story is at the same location as the immediately preceding event, then the location does not need to be repeated, unless for clarity or readability (e.g., emphasis). Therefore, if you find that you keep repeating the same spatial information at different time points, you could evaluate the spatial information for omission.

(b) Facts relevant to the case: Undisputed and disputed facts, and those with uncertain disputation. Writers of legal documents sometimes include too many factual details that are not relevant to the case and are not otherwise needed for coherence, clarity, or readability. Which facts do you retain? It does not matter whether the facts are undisputed or disputed, or whether they have uncertain disputation. The facts that you decide to retain need to be relevant, need to help the information cohere and be clear, and need to assist in creating a readable text.

Relevancy. Are the included facts relevant to the law, such as to one of the *prima facie* elements, from either your or your opposing party's perspective? If yes, you should probably include the facts; if not, you should consider omitting them. For example, in sentence 5 of Table 33, the information *the terrible but all-too-predictable* is not an undisputed, a disputed, or an uncertain fact; it is opinion attached to the fact *consequence of Exxon's behavior*, and this opinion occurs in a fact section. Therefore, it could be omitted.

Coherence, clarity, and readability. Do the included facts give coherence or clarity to the story? Do they help create a readable text? Once mentioned, facts can be repeated to lead readers from one sentence or paragraph to another. For example, in Table 33, sentence 3 begins with the useful transition *shortly after his reinstatement*, which repeats information from sentence 2, namely that Hazelwood *was reinstated*. For another example, sentence 6 repeats the fact that Exxon knew the captain was an alcoholic, in the phrasing *Exxon's known alcoholic captain*. Repeated information is not always problematic (see Strategy 30 and Strategy 4); it can be useful in providing transitions. However, if not useful, you should consider omitting the information.

If you are unsure of the disputation of a certain fact, that does not necessarily affect whether or not you retain the fact. The facts you retain still need to be relevant to the law, and they need to help clarify the story or help it cohere or assist in the readability of the text. If they do not achieve these purposes, you can omit them.

3. Legal argument. Application of law to facts comprises legal argumentation. Legal argumentation is complex, and the discussion here is necessarily incomplete. Briefly, good legal argumentation requires that your legal positions (claims) be logical—that is, that your claims be reasonable deductions given the facts of the case; that you identify your claims and the relevant facts that substantiate your claims, given the relevant law; that you identify your opposing party's claims and problems in their substantiation, in terms of the relevant facts and the relevant law; that you identify law that does not substantiate your position; and why the court should take particular action, given the relevant facts and the relevant law. If your legal argument has other information, you can consider omitting that information.

Table 33 presents the section **Summary Argument** that precedes the section **Argument** in an *amicus curiae*. This example illustrates features of a legal argument, and types of legal-argumentation information are identified in the right-hand column. Since this passage has no extraneous, non-legal-argumentation information, no content can be eliminated here. To shorten this text, we need to turn to the other 34 strategies.

4. Conclusion. In a legal document, information that you can omit—or at least significantly reduce—is factual information repeated in a conclusion. A conclusion that just repeats an assortment of facts independent of an application of relevant law to the facts can be shortened by the elimination of the repeated facts. At the other extreme, a conclusion that contains no substantive information to support the major claim is useless, such as the conclusion in the following example:

Example 36
CONCLUSION
The judgment of the Court of Appeals should be affirmed.

From Doc. 5. Total word count: 11, Total character count: 68

When shortening a legal document to meet length constraints, you need to make sure that you do not strip a section of necessary content. Example 36 illustrates the type of section that can result when you are desperate for space and over-edit for content. In such a case, it may be more useful to reapply Strategies 1–34 in this book to the entire document than to just shorten the conclusion.

Table 33. Retaining Necessary Information and Omitting Nonessential Information.

From Doc. 5. Total line count: 49, Total word count: 368, Total character count: 2333

STATEMENT

1. [1]*For many years*, Exxon knew that its employee, Joseph Hazelwood, had a drinking problem that interfered with his work on Exxon supertankers. Pet. App. 63a-64a; 121a. [2]*In 1985*, after Exxon received reports of Hazelwood's drinking problem, Hazelwood went to an alcohol treatment program *that lasted 28 days, after which* Hazelwood was reinstated to command supertankers. Pet. App. 63a; *see* Pet. App. 121a. [3]*Shortly after his reinstatement*, however, his superiors at Exxon received reports that Hazelwood had returned to drinking. Pet. App. 64a; 121a. [4]Despite many such reports, Exxon left Hazelwood in command of the EXXON VALDEZ. Pet. App. 64a; 121a.

[5]*On March 24, 1989*, the **terrible but all-too-predictable** consequence of Exxon's behavior happened. [6]Although the supertanker was freshly loaded with 53 million gallons of crude oil, Exxon's known alcoholic captain—the only officer aboard licensed to navigate through the difficult parts of Prince William Sound—was drunk and left his post. *See* Pet. App. 61a-64a; 120a-122a. [7]The fatigued Third Mate, who was not licensed to steer the ship in those waters, was left in charge and *eventually* the ship ran into Bligh Reef. Pet. App. 63a-64a; 120a-121a. [8]As Exxon acknowledged and stipulated to in the district court, Hazelwood "was negligent in leaving the bridge of the vessel on the night of the grounding, [his] negligence was a legal cause of the oil spill, and . . . the Exxon defendants are responsible for this act of negligence." JA212.

The grounding of the EXXON VALDEZ spilled
nearly 11 million gallons of oil into Prince William
Sound. Pet. App. 64a; 122a. The oil *eventually* spread
across several hundred linear miles and impacted
over 10,000 square miles of the surrounding coastal
saltwater ecosystem, including well over 1,000 miles
of coastline. *See* Exxon Valdez Oil Spill Trustee
Council, *History,* http://www.evostc.state.ak.us/History/
PWSmap.cfm. This astounding spill is one of the
largest spills *to date* in American waters, *United
States v. Locke*, 529 U.S. 89, 94 (2000); JONATHAN L.
RAMSEUR, CONGRESSIONAL RESEARCH SERVICE, OIL
SPILLS IN U.S. COASTAL WATERS at CRS-1 (2007), and
"it is widely considered the number one spill worldwide
in terms of damage to the environment." *See*
Exxon Valdez Oil Spill Trustee Council, *History FAQ,*
http://www.evostc.state.ak
.us/history/faq.cfm.

Table 33. Specifying the Legal Argument.

From Doc. 5. Total line count: 21, Total word count: 157, Total character count: 968

SUMMARY OF ARGUMENT

[1]After almost two decades of litigation, Exxon has asked this Court to review the punitive damages awarded as a result of Exxon's reckless conduct that led to the grounding of the EXXON VALDEZ. [2]Although Exxon has presented this as a complicated case, the issues are straightforward.

[3]This Court should affirm the award because the rule applied by the courts below comports with the realities of the modern maritime industry, it is consistent with how other industries are treated in similar circumstances, and its results are fair to all maritime businesses. [4]Moreover, this particular award, which amounts to average punitive damages of about $75,000 per plaintiff, is reasonable and consistent with the purposes for punitive damages. [5]Finally, even if Exxon had not waived its Clean Water Act argument, that Act poses no bar to recovery of punitive damages for harms to the private economic interests of the more than 30,000 plaintiffs resulting from the EXXON VALDEZ oil spill.

Story, facts

Position/claim

Requested court action

3 categories of support for the request

Position/claim

Opposing position/claim

Position/claim

Index